THE TIME TRAVELERS' HANDBOOK

A WILD, WACKY, AND WOOLY ADVENTURE THROUGH HISTORY!

By Lottie Stride • Illustrated by Dusan Pavlic

FEIWEL AND FRIENDS • NEW YORK

Edited by Sally Pilkington
History Consultant: Dr. Kelvin Meek
With thanks to Alanna Skuse

A Feiwel and Friends Book
An Imprint of Macmillan

THE TIME TRAVELERS' HANDBOOK. Text and illustrations
copyright © 2009 by Buster Books. All rights reserved.
Printed in September 2009 in the United States of America
by Quebecor World, Fairfield, Pennsylvania. For information,
address Feiwel and Friends, 175 Fifth Avenue,
New York, N.Y. 10010.

Library of Congress Cataloging-in-Publication Data Available

ISBN: 978-0-312-58089-6

Book design by Zoe Quayle

Originally published in Great Britain by Buster Books,
an imprint of Michael O'Mara Books Limited

Feiwel and Friends logo designed by Filomena Tuosto

First U.S. Edition: 2009

10 9 8 7 6 5 4 3 2 1

www.feiwelandfriends.com

CONTENTS

WELCOME TO TIME TRAVEL

Welcome. Your very first journey through time is about to begin.

This is your time travel (TT) handset. It's an amazing and essential piece of equipment for all time travelers. In this book, you are going to use its LEAP button, which will catapult you back to specific points in time and places in the world. When you arrive, check the handset's screen to find out what year you have landed in.

TIME TRAVEL DOS AND DON'TS

To help you get the most out of your time travels, here are some dos and don'ts:

- **Do** take very good care of your TT handset. When not in use, keep it in a secure pocket or, even better, attach it to your belt. If you lose it, there is NO WAY BACK HOME. The handset is state-of-the-art technology, so it is pretty unlikely you will be able to pick up a new one in Ancient Egypt.

- **Don't** worry if you feel a bit strange or dizzy upon landing the first few times. It's perfectly normal. Not everyone enjoys the sensation of whizzing through time right away. Like most things, time travel gets easier each time you do it.

• **Do** treat any people you meet on your travels with respect. They may not have computers, or even metal tools, but that doesn't mean they're stupid—they're just living in an earlier time than you. Asking them if they like football or hip-hop, or even if you can borrow their cell phone will make you very unpopular, and they will probably think you are totally crazy.

• **Don't** hesitate to hit the large red EJECT button in the center of your handset any time you feel threatened or scared. Don't hang around—the past can be a dangerous place.

Activating the EJECT button will shoot you out of harm's way, then fast-forward you back home.

Unfortunately, the EJECT button will only send you back to the present day. It won't get you out of hot water if your parents have just discovered a mess in your bedroom. You will have to deal with that yourself.

• **Do** speak normally. Your handset is equipped with a state-of-the-art program called BlabberSpeak. BlabberSpeak automatically adjusts to the language of the time and place you land in. With BlabberSpeak enabled, you will be able to both understand and speak to the people you meet on your travels as long as you are holding the handset, or it is attached to your belt.

• **Don't** panic. Your clothes will travel through time with you. You won't find yourself stark naked and chatting to Henry VIII.

WARNING

Do not try to change the course of history, no matter how tempting it is. Time travel is not to be used for personal gain, other than for gaining knowledge.

Going back in time to buy a lottery ticket after finding out this week's numbers is strictly forbidden. Your TT handset will know about it and take immediate action by transporting you back to Victorian times and setting you to work as a chimney sweep (see pages 26 to 29). It will not return you home until it is convinced you have seen the error of your ways.

• **Do** breathe freely. The TT handset is equipped with an ImmunoShield. This helps protect you from catching the bugs of the past, and also keeps you from giving modern coughs and colds to people you meet on your travels.

• **Do** consult this book before you go, and keep it with you during your visit. It will provide you with top tips and essential time-tourist information, highlighting must-see sights and things that are in your best interests to avoid.

Now you're ready to go.

Take a deep breath and press the LEAP button.

Good luck, and enjoy your travels!

HOW TO BEAT THE MAYAN AT BALL

AD 800

The roar of a crowd brings you to your senses and you find you are standing in the middle of what looks like some kind of ball court. You are in the area of the world now known as Southern Mexico and Guatemala, and the roaring crowd are all Mayan—an Indian people famed for their buildings, astronomy, and ball games. The good news is a Mayan ball game is about to begin. The bad news is that this game is much more than just an exciting team sport—it can be very dangerous. The outcome of the game can determine whether the players live or die.

LET'S PLAY BALL

The ball court you are standing in is shaped like a capital letter I, with high sides decorated with elaborate carvings. The high sides help to keep the ball in play.

For the game itself, you are going to need to put on some equipment to protect you from injury. The ball is made of solid rubber. It can weigh almost nine pounds and is hard enough to break your bones. So make sure you strap on some padded shin, knee, and forearm protectors made from animal skin. Think yourself lucky though—the ball was sometimes made from a human skull wrapped in strips of rubber to make it bounce well.

Put on your feathered headdress and you are ready to play ball. You look a-Maya-zing—as do the other members of your team who enter the court wearing their finest animal skins, feather headdresses, and jewelry.

MAYAN RULES

Now this is the tricky part: Historians aren't exactly sure how this game was played. So, you are going to have to keep your wits about you. What previous time travelers do know, however, is that you should try really hard to help your team win, because the losers are often sacrificed to the gods.

Take a look at the end of the court. You will notice that there is a stone ring, just large enough for the ball to fit through. It is probably a wise move to aim for that. Make sure you are whacking the ball in the right direction—own goals aren't good no matter which century you are in.

GET IN SOME PRACTICE

You will need:

• an open space • shin pads/elbow pads/any kind of helmet
• a soft soccer ball or beach ball • two hoops or buckets

Put a hoop at each end of your playing area about eight yards apart. If you don't have hoops, place a bucket at each end.

Get a group of friends together and divide into two teams with at least two players on each side. Then put on your protective gear (you shouldn't really need this if your ball is soft enough, but it will help you get into the spirit of the game if you do). Jaguar-skin skirts are optional!

The aim of the game is to get the ball into your bucket. So, decide which team is going to aim for which goal. Then, determine with the toss of a coin which team will start the game. The winner of the toss starts with the ball.

It is thought that the Mayan players were not allowed to use their feet to move the ball. They had to whack it with their knees, arms, or hips. You are not allowed to kick, catch, or throw the ball, other than with clenched fists. To begin, the ball can be headed, punched, kneed, or chested to a player on the same team. The team with the most goals after 10 minutes wins.

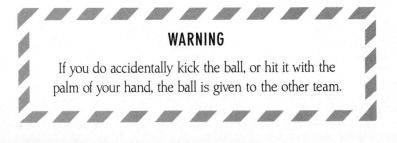

WARNING

If you do accidentally kick the ball, or hit it with the palm of your hand, the ball is given to the other team.

HOW TO BEAT THE SPANISH ARMADA

The wind is blasting your ears, and you are swaying back and forth like part of a circus act. You've landed in the crow's nest of an English warship. Unfortunately, a crow's nest is a little lookout platform three-quarters of the way up the ship's mast.

All around you other ships are racing through the waves. Your ship is part of an English fleet chasing the mighty warships of a fleet known as the Spanish Armada away from the English coast.

TOP TACTICS

You're spotted, and the sailors suspect you of being a stowaway. They take you to the commander, Sir Charles Howard. Unfortunately, he has been known to keelhaul rebellious sailors, having them dragged beneath the ship by a rope. They would be cut to ribbons by the barnacles below. Luckily, he's in a good mood. After months of fierce fighting, the Spanish are on the run. So, he's quite happy to quaff a tot of rum and tell you his tactics:

• Sir Charles is using fast, nimble ships. The Spanish galleons are much bigger, and when it comes to turning, they are a lot slower.

• The English crews are experienced sailors, whereas the Spanish have packed their ships with soldiers. The Spanish plan is to get close to the enemy ships and board them, but the English sail their ships too well to let the Spanish get near.

• Sir Charles is making good use of cannons. The English go in really close, attack the Spanish from the sides, and fire at short range. They have better long-range guns, too, which means they can fire more accurately at the Spanish from farther away.

• Sir Charles's commanders have had a brainstorm. One night, they set eight of the oldest ships afire. The wind blew them into the Spanish fleet and the Spanish were forced to sail off up the coast to get away from them.

LIFE AFLOAT

Life on board seems so exciting, you decide to join the crew for supper. Unfortunately, first on the menu is salted meat and soggy crackers with little bugs called weevils in them. As night falls, a crew of 40 men eating, fighting, and sleeping in the same clothes for months on end does not make belowdecks smell good. After one night in the dark, damp, crowded, and smelly ship, you will never complain about sharing a room with your brother again.

WHAT 'KNOT' TO DO

In the morning, a sailor tells you Sir Charles has insisted you
earn your keep. He shows you how to tie some essential knots,
including a bowline, which is used to attach a rope to a post
or railing.

1. Make a small loop a little way along the
rope. It helps if you imagine the loop is a
rabbit hole, the tip of the rope is the rabbit
itself, and the rest of the rope is a tree.

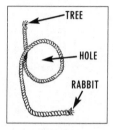

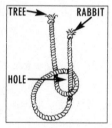

2. Feed the rabbit up
through the hole as
shown.

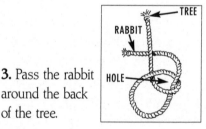

3. Pass the rabbit
around the back
of the tree.

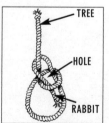

4. Pass the rabbit
down into the hole.

5. Pull it tight.

HOW TO MAKE SILK IN ANCIENT CHINA

700 BC

Yuck! All around you are wooden trays packed with pale, grayish, squishy-looking worms. There are millions of them—munching on leaves and wriggling about in their own droppings.

You've landed in Ancient China, right in the middle of a silkworm farm. Beside you, a girl is fishing a silkworm out of one of the trays. Her name is Mei Ying and she tells you that the worms are not actually worms at all, but caterpillars of the silk moth. The caterpillars are eating mulberry leaves, and have been eating nonstop for about six weeks. They hatched from tiny little eggs and have shed their skin four times to become the fat caterpillars they are now.

Mei Ying picks one up to show it to you up close. It is shooting what looks like little threads out of its mouth and she tells you that this is silk. The caterpillar is making a cocoon.

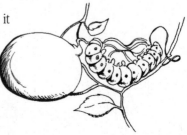

11

Mei Ying puts the caterpillar into a wooden frame next to lots of others that have already finished their cocoons. She says that the silk is actually the caterpillar's hardened saliva, or spit. Each caterpillar wraps itself in more than a half mile of silk. She holds up a finished cocoon and explains the caterpillar inside is busy turning itself into a moth. Unfortunately, none of these caterpillars is ever going to be a moth.

She leads you to a large pan of boiling water that contains lots of the cocoons bobbing about like white cotton balls. When the cocoons are thrown in, the caterpillar inside dies, and the thread softens and is easier to work with. Mei Ying says the cocoons are ready for her mother to work on. She gets some chopsticks

and starts fishing cocoons out of the pan and putting them in a basket. This looks very easy, but when you try, they keep dropping back in.

Mei Ying hears a noise and asks you to hide—she will be in great danger if she is found talking to you. The process of spinning the caterpillar silk into thread and weaving it into cloth is a closely guarded secret. The Chinese are the only people in the world who know how to do it, and they make lots of money from trading their fine cloth all over the world. Revealing the secret is punishable by death. From your hiding place, you see Mei Ying's mother come in. She takes a cocoon from the basket and sits at a kind of spinning wheel. She examines the cocoon, looking for the end of the silk thread. When she finds it, she uses a silk reel to unravel the cocoon.

As you watch, you find it hard to believe that little fat caterpillars can produce so much thread. Mei Ying has told you that even though a single caterpillar can produce more than a half mile of thread, the thread is so fine that it can take up to 100 cocoons to make a single scarf.

Next, Mei Ying's mother twists 10 to 12 silk threads together to form a stronger thread. These can then be dyed different colors and used for embroidery or woven into cloth. The wonderful silk cloth produced will be packed and transported along a route known as the Old Silk Road (see pages 111 to 113).

HOW TO HUNT A MAMMOTH

Traveling thousands of years back in time can be a bumpy ride. You find yourself crash-landing right in the middle of a group of muscular, hairy people. What's more—they're all armed! Every single one of them is holding a wooden spear with a pointed tip that looks very sharp. These hairy people are called Neanderthals—a species of primitive human.

Resist the temptation to push EJECT on your TT handset. It's not you the hairy hunters are after—it's a mammoth. Mammoths are a type of hairy elephant with long curved tusks that are extinct today. You've landed in one of the top Neanderthal mammoth-hunting teams. So, get ready for your first mammoth hunt.

A MAMMOTH TASK

One of the guys hands you a spear, and points to the ground. There's a trail of enormous footprints on the ground, and an enormous pile of steaming mammoth poop—sure signs a mammoth is nearby.

When it comes to hunting, a mammoth has all the advantages except one— you and the team have bigger brains. There are various ways to outwit a mammoth. You could

build a huge pit, disguise it with leaves and branches, and then herd the mammoth into it. Or, if you find a weak mammoth, you could use spears, stones, or poisoned darts to finish it off.

Today, your team is hoping to use the mammoth's own size against it. They plan to drive it into a nearby swamp. Mammoths can grow to over 10 feet tall and weigh more than 15,000 pounds! Their tusks are sharp and can be 10 feet long. This much mammoth is a lot easier to kill once it's floundering in swampy water!

First, the team quietly and stealthily surrounds the mammoth, leaving just one gap for it to escape through—right into the muddy swamp. Then, at the team leader's signal, you all charge at the mammoth, shouting, yelling, and swinging flaming sticks.

Be careful to keep your footing so you don't get trampled. The panicking mammoth will look for a way out, and if it sees a gap, it will make a run for it.

HUNTING HINTS

Mammoth hunting is risky and difficult, but there are things you can do to give you and your team a greater chance of success:

• Always make sure to stay downwind of a mammoth. That way, you can smell the mammoth (and a mammoth is easy to smell), but the mammoth can't smell you.

• Make as little noise as possible when moving in on a mammoth. Move slowly and tread very carefully. Keep your weight on your back foot while you use your front foot to check for sticks or anything else that might make a noise. Only move your weight onto your front foot when you're sure you can do so quietly and without tripping.

• If the mammoth stops feeding, raises its trunk high above its head, and swivels it about, it's bad news. Your mammoth has nostrils at the end of its trunk, and those nostrils may have picked up your scent.

• If you are sure your mammoth has spotted you—don't panic. Top mammoth hunters never panic. Instead, freeze. Your mammoth may never have seen a human before, and it may not know what you're planning. If you stay still, your mammoth might relax and go back to its feeding, because feeding was probably a full-time job for a mammoth. Like elephants, mammoths probably needed to feed for up to 18 hours a day.

• Above all, stick with your team. One on one, you wouldn't stand a chance against a mammoth. It's huge—a fully grown mammoth weighs over 150 times more than you do.

HOW TO MAKE PAPYRUS IN ANCIENT EGYPT

2500 BC

You've landed behind a thick clump of reeds beside the Nile River in Egypt. No one has spotted you—and make sure you keep it that way, because what you're about to see is a closely guarded secret. It is 2500 BC, and the Ancient Egyptians are the only people in the whole world who have figured out how to make writing scrolls from a special kind of reed called papyrus. They make a lot of money selling these scrolls, and they don't want anyone else to know how they make them. If they see you, they might think you're a spy, and who knows what they'll do to you.

You might want to look out for crocodiles as well. They are very common in this part of the world and like nothing more than lurking in reeds, just like the ones you are hiding in.

MAKING PAPYRUS

You spot a group of people pulling up papyrus reeds along the banks of the Nile. You follow them as they leave the riverbank, but stay well hidden to watch them at work making scrolls.

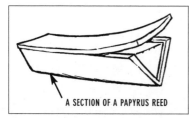

A SECTION OF A PAPYRUS REED

Papyrus reeds have a tough outside layer that is peeled off. The workers keep this part and use it to make other things, like baskets and sandals.

Inside the reed is a sticky stalk that they slice into strips. They pound these strips flat with heavy blocks of wood and then soak them in water from the river for up to three days.

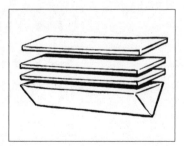

Luckily, you don't have to wait that long. Another group of men is working on strips that are ready. Using pieces of wood that look like rolling pins, they squish out all the water and make the strips flat.

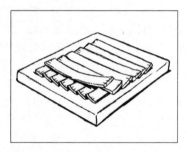

Next, they start laying the strips out, each one overlapping the one before it a tiny bit. The first layer is horizontal, then they add a vertical layer on top. The strips contain a natural sticky gum, so they glue themselves together as they dry.

To dry the papyrus, the men place sheets made of linen and felt over it. The sheets are then squashed between two boards in a press that squeezes it all together. The men will keep replacing the linen sheets over the next few days.

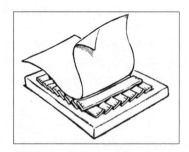

You see a pile of finished papyrus being joined together, end to end, to make a big roll, about 33 yards long. You also see the man who's joining them look up. He's spotted you—it's time to go.

HOW TO BE EVACUATED IN WORLD WAR II

It is 1939 and Britain is at war with Germany. You've landed on a train in England. It is packed with children, all waving out of the window as the train pulls out of the station.

A boy about your own age makes a space for you next to him. His name is Thomas.

Thomas tells you he is from a city called Coventry in England, and that he and all of the kids in his school are being sent to the countryside because it's too dangerous for them to stay in the city. This is called evacuation and it is happening all over the country. All the major cities are sending their school-age children out to the countryside, where it is hoped they will be safe. The Germans have a big air force and most people think they'll start dropping bombs on the big cities soon.

Thomas is skinny-looking and scratches his head as if he has lice. He has a label on his jacket with his name and address on it, a small suitcase, and a gas mask. You ask to try the gas mask on. It smells rubbery and makes your face feel hot and horrible. Thomas doesn't mind, he knows it could save his life if the Germans drop poison gas on everybody. He asks why you don't have one, and why you don't have a label.

Thomas seems very nervous. He can't decide whether to be excited or homesick. He has never been out of Coventry before. He is leaving his home and his parents, and doesn't know who he will be living with, or how long he will be gone. He is worried about his parents, too. His dad is away fighting and his mother is still in Coventry.

TOO MANY CHILDREN

After a couple of nervous hours on the train with only one sandwich to keep you going, you're tired and hungry, but the day's not over yet. Once the train stops, all the children march into a big village hall. There is a lot of confusion and you see a crowd of adults staring.

People living in the area have agreed to take children into their homes. The grown-ups are looking around and choosing the children they want to take, but there doesn't seem to be enough grown-ups for the number of children looking for homes.

A woman holding a clipboard is scratching her head and looking very worried. You and Thomas hope you won't be left until last.

TOP TIPS FOR GETTING PICKED

It is important to be chosen by nice people who will look after you well. Some people don't want children living with them, but if there are still evacuees left over, officers can order people to take in a child. They will get a fine if they don't. So, here are some ways to improve your chances of getting picked.

- **Do** make yourself look neat—smooth down unruly hair and straighten your clothes. Imagine that you were for sale. Would anyone want to buy you with a dirty nose and your jacket buttoned up all wrong?

- **Do** speak only when spoken to—and be polite, answering questions with "Yes, sir" or "Yes, ma'am."

- **Don't** scratch—the villagers might think you have fleas and will not want to take you into their homes.

CHOSEN!

You and your friend duck your heads as an extra-grumpy-looking man with a big stick comes past. Luckily, he passes right by and then another couple, with smiling faces, come along. They take one look at Thomas and say he needs a good meal. They approach the woman with the clipboard and sort out the paperwork.

You had better get out of here quickly. Not only will your name not be on the list of children they were expecting, you don't even have a label. So you quickly say good-bye and good luck to Thomas, and press EJECT.

AD 1851

HOW TO JOIN THE AMERICAN GOLD RUSH

Splash! The good news is you have landed in the new state of California, on the west coast of the U.S.A. The bad news is you have landed in a river.

In front of you is a man holding a pan half in, half out of the water and he is swirling around what looks like mud and pebbles. The man's staring down at the pan very hard.

All of a sudden, he gives a shout, throws his hat in the air—and that's when you see that there is something interesting in the pan after all. A small chunk of metal is glittering in the dirt at the bottom of his pan. Gold!

THE FORTY-NINERS

When he has stopped jumping for joy, he introduces himself as Nathaniel. Gold was discovered in this river in March 1848. At first, people didn't believe the news—they thought it was just a government scheme to get folks to move west to California from their comfortable homes in the east. Now, thousands of people have rushed here to strike it rich.

They call it "gold fever." People seem to have gone crazy—obsessed with the idea of finding gold. The people that came here are called "Forty-niners" because many of them arrived in 1849. Since then, new towns have been springing up.

A FLASH IN THE PAN

Your friend is one of the lucky Forty-niners. He came early when there was still gold to be had. Back then, he was panning nearly $100 a day. He brought along his whole family, selling everything they had to get here—their house, their furniture, even their dog. They traveled more than 2,000 miles across the continent.

Now, Nathaniel's noticed he is finding far less gold. It's running out. Today's find was his first in weeks. But more people are arriving every day. They spend up to 10 hours a day, standing in freezing water panning for gold, but find nothing.

MAKING MONEY

Along with all the people looking for gold, known as prospectors, others have arrived—merchants and con men. They are hated. They make their money by buying up every bit of gold-panning equipment in the area, and then selling it at many times the original price. Others charge huge amounts for food and supplies. Those prospectors who do not find gold can't afford food at these incredible prices—some even starve to death.

PANNING FOR GOLD

Nathaniel is not too downcast. One Forty-niner pulled a nugget the size of a turkey egg out of this river—right where you are standing, he tells you. He offers you a pan, and shows you how to pan for gold.

1. Fill your pan about half full with the mixture of dirt and gravel that has collected at the banks of the river.

2. Gently put your pan beneath the surface and fill it with water. Take it out and break up all the muddy clumps with your hands to loosen all the dirt—and perhaps gold.

3. Drain away some of the water and take out twigs and rocks. Tip the pan beneath the surface of the water gently to fill the pan again.

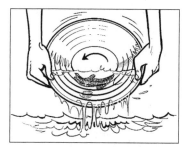

4. Now, swirl the pan near the surface of the water. Gold is heavy, so this should make it sink towards the bottom. Be gentle and take care not to slosh any dirt out of your pan.

5. As you keep shaking, the lighter dirt rises up. Lift the pan out of the water, and tilt the front down. Water will run off the edge of the pan, taking the lighter dirt at the top with it. Any gold should be in the bottom of the pan.

You keep swirling and tipping away the dirt for what feels like ages. Nathaniel finishes his pan and fills up to start again. You are about to do the same when . . . you see it: something glinting in the bottom of the pan. It might not be the size of a turkey egg, but you've done it—you've struck gold!

Unfortunately, Nathaniel reminds you that he has staked a claim to this bit of river. That means the gold is his. He gives you a slice of his wife's homemade pie instead—hmmm . . .

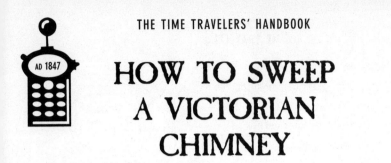

HOW TO SWEEP A VICTORIAN CHIMNEY

Watch out! You are about to be run over by a horse and carriage speeding toward you. You leap out of the way onto the sidewalk and take a look around. You have landed in the middle of a London street during the reign of Queen Victoria.

There are some fancy houses on either side of the road with steps going up to the main door. The houses are four to five stories high, with spiked iron fences to keep people out.

As well as the steps going up to the main door, you see that there are steps going down to another door that is far less fancy.

You see a man emerging out of one of these doors. He is with two boys slightly younger than you. They are very thin and have no shoes on. Their faces are completely black with dirt and you notice that their eyes are red and watery. The street is very busy and everybody seems to be in a hurry, but you are worried about the boys and decide to go and speak to them.

CLIMBING BOYS

The smaller of the two boys has clearly been crying and the other is trying to calm him down. You ask what is wrong and find out that they are brothers and are both working as "climbing boys," otherwise known as chimney sweeps. They have just been cleaning the chimneys in the house you saw them leaving.

The younger boy is upset because his feet are hurting so much, he is finding it hard to walk. His older brother explains that this is his fault. He says that while they were working, their boss complained that they were taking too long. The older boy was sent up the chimney to make his little brother work faster. To hurry him along, he had to prod the soles of his brother's feet with hot pins. What's worse, they are now late for their next chimney and their boss is angry and will dock their pay.

Feeling sorry for the brothers, you offer to help out. You are a bit bigger than the youngest, but are willing to give chimney sweeping a try. The smaller boy stops crying, happy to be off the hook and the older boy quickly gives you some tips.

TOP SWEEP TIPS

• Don't go to the front door of the fancy houses like the ones on this street. You will be asked to go in the tradesman's entrance. Customers don't like sooty sweeps tramping dirt through the house.

• When you are inside the house, don't touch anything except the chimney. Not only do you not want to make things dirty, but you also want to avoid being accused of stealing anything. If you are, you risk being sent to a horrid Victorian prison.

• Make sure you put lots of sheets around the fireplace to collect all the soot. If you make a mess, you will be punished and could be forced to clean the next chimney naked!

• When up a chimney, hold the cleaning brush in one hand and push your knees and elbows against the walls to help you climb. Shuffle up, one knee and elbow at a time, sweeping the brush ahead of you.

• Get to the top as quick as you can, or your friend will be sent after you to poke you in the feet with hot pins.

• Don't complain. These boys are lucky to have jobs. With no parents, they have nowhere else to go and would be left on the street to starve. In Victorian England, children as young as five work in factories or underground in mines.

HEALTH WARNING

• The inside of the chimney has lots of sharp bits of brick that can hurt your elbows, knees, and feet. If the soot and dirt get into cuts and scratches, they can become infected and start oozing pus.

• Try to keep your eyes shut. The soot is full of toxic chemicals that will make them sore and itchy.

• Try to retire young. Being a chimney sweep is very bad for your health. The soot will damage your lungs and leave your face permanently dirty. Lugging around big sacks of soot will hurt your back and leave you with hunched shoulders. When you get bigger, you will no longer be able to climb the chimney and may be too injured to work anywhere else.

After climbing up only one chimney, you decide this is not a career for you and that it is time to get out of there. You whiz back to the present to take a long soak in the bathtub. It's a shame your two new friends can't do the same.

HOW TO COMPETE AT THE ANCIENT OLYMPICS

You have landed on a running track in a huge stadium that is packed with noisy spectators on all sides. It's day one of the Ancient Olympiad, the biggest festival in Ancient Greece, celebrated in honor of Zeus, king of the Greek gods.

Just like the Olympics in modern times, the Olympiad is held every four years, but always here in the city of Olympia. The festival is considered so important that wars between cities are stopped so that the athletes can travel safely to the games.

FIGHTING FIT

Nervously, you line up with a group of boys who are about your age and size. They're all warming up for a 192-metre (210-yard) sprint from one end of the stadium to the other.

The Ancient Greeks think being fit and healthy is very important. All boys in Ancient Greece do a lot of athletic training, and these are the cream of the crop. They've been training hard for months in a place called the *palaistra*, the wrestling school. They have been eating healthily and working hard—which means you're up against some tough competition.

As you are waiting for the starter's orders, follow these top tips:

• Try not to let the butterflies in your stomach bother you. They'll go away as soon as you start running. They're caused by your body producing a chemical called adrenaline. This is completely natural and will give you a burst of speed across the stadium.

• Don't worry about not having your running shoes with you. Take a look around. No one else is wearing any—in fact, they aren't wearing anything at all! Ancient Greek men and boys trained and competed completely naked. So strip down and get ready to run.

• Try to block out the roaring crowd and go through the race in your head. Imagine yourself being super-speedy and think how good you'll feel when you cross that finish line first.

WHAT NEXT?

The downside is that if you win, you shouldn't expect a medal. Ancient Greeks didn't do medals. Winners get a crown made out of olive branches.

The good bit is Olympic winners are celebrities and are greeted by cheering crowds when they return home to their towns and cities. In the meantime, while you are in Olympia, you can expect some nice free meals and front row seats at the theater. You may even get a statue built in your honor.

WHILE YOU WAIT

If you win any of the races, you'll have to hang around for your prize, because the Ancient Olympiad goes on for five days and the prizes are all given out at the end.

Here are a few things you can do while you're waiting:

• What better way to while away the hours than taking in a chariot race or two? There are two- and four-horse events, as well as a cart and mule race. Chariot races are very exciting with up to 40 chariots jostling for first place during the 12 laps. You might not want to sit in the front row for this one, though. Crashes are common and you don't want to get trampled by a runaway horse.

• For a seriously tough sport, why not watch some boxing? The boxers don't wear gloves like modern boxers, they just wrap bits of leather around their hands, leaving their fingers sticking out.

The boxing matches don't have rounds; each fight continues until someone gives up or loses consciousness. Watch out for a man named Theagenes of Thassos—he is said to be this year's favorite. At the age of nine, he was so strong that he managed to tear a bronze statue of a god off its base and carry it home.

BOYS ONLY

Sorry, girls. The Ancient Olympiad is for boys and men only. Girls aren't even allowed to watch the games, and any girl caught trying to is punished.

Don't worry, a separate festival in honor of Zeus' wife, Hera, is held here in Olympia. It is called the *Heraia* and takes place every four years, too. The *Heraia* is the Ancient Greek girls' chance to show off their running skills. To compete, girls wear tunics cut just above the knee and draped over their left shoulder.

HOW TO PAINT A CAVE

17,000 BC

It's pitch-dark. You can't see a thing, and you have no idea where you've landed. Luckily, all TT handsets are equipped with an emergency illuminator switch. You press it, and at once, the room is flooded with light. But it's not a room at all. You are inside an enormous cave, and there's an incredible painting of two huge gray bulls on the wall in front of you.

You walk farther on and see wall after wall covered in paintings of huge animals. Up ahead, you see light glimmering. Follow the light, and you find yourself in another huge cave about 100 feet long. There's someone in here hard at work, sketching the outline of a leaping horse on the cave wall.

You're in the Lascaux Cave, in the Pyrenees Mountains in France. The cave is one of a series of caves and tunnels filled with what will become some of the most famous Stone Age cave paintings in the world. The gallery you're in right now is known as the Painted Gallery, and has walls 11 feet high.

SHEDDING SOME LIGHT

The glimmering is coming from a flat sandstone lamp with a hollowed out dip at one end. The artist has filled this dip with something that is burning brightly enough for you to see what he's doing.

The paintings you have seen are all in browns, blacks, reds, and grays. The artist is using paints made from minerals and natural

substances. Some rocks contain a lot of iron oxide; this substance gives a rusty red color. Rocks containing a mineral called manganese oxide give a strong black color. The artist shows you how he grinds rocks down to a powder and mixes the powder with either water or grease to make it easier to apply to the cave walls.

PAINT YOUR OWN CAVE

The artist hands you his painting implement and now it's your turn to try painting a mammoth.

You will need:
• paper • a pencil • crayons
• a cup of cold dark tea • a large paintbrush

First, sketch out your design on paper using a pencil. Don't worry if you aren't a great artist. Cave paintings tend to be very simple. The more simple yours is, the more real it will look. Why not draw a mammoth following these simple steps?

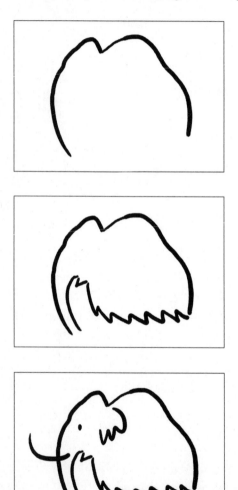

1. First draw the mammoth's outline— with a hump for its head and one for its back (it should look like a fat M shape.)

2. Add the bottom of the mammoth's trunk and its mouth. Don't forget the shaggy fur.

3. Next, draw the ears, eye and tusks . . .

4. . . . and some legs.

Using a large paintbrush, cover your paper with cold tea to give it that authentic ancient-cave look. You should still be able to see your drawing through the tea. Don't worry if your paper wrinkles.

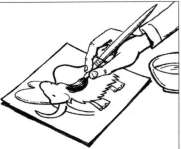

Now, you're ready to go over your mammoth with crayons. The cave painters didn't have a lot of colors to choose from, so stick to reds, orangey yellows, browns, and blacks for an authentic look.

Top Tip: Why not think bigger? Get hold of a roll of newsprint paper and create a long row of animals along one wall of your bedroom. Add lots of stick men holding spears. Don't draw right on your walls. You may think it's the best way to relive your cave painting experience, but chances are your mother will get angrier than a mammoth with a spear in its side.

HOW TO PULL OFF THE GREAT ESCAPE

You find yourself in a wooden hut among a crowd of men. They are huddled together, talking in whispers. You have landed in Germany during World War II, in a camp full of prisoners of war. The men around you are prisoners from the British air force, and they are about to embark on a daring breakout.

You feel a sense of urgency in the air; you hear it in the whispered, panicky conversations; you see it in the eyes of the lookouts by the door who are checking right and left for German soldiers.

UNDER THEIR FEET

The Germans think their camp, called Stalag Luft III, is impossible to escape from. They're wrong—76 prisoners are about to do just that, making their escape through a tunnel right under the Germans' feet.

In front of you is the mouth of a tunnel and it's uncovered. One after another, men are disappearing into it as fast as they can. The escape has taken months of planning and preparation. Now, the moment has come. Before you know it, it's your turn to duck through the trapdoor. You are part of the Great Escape!

THE PLAN SO FAR

The escape was masterminded by a man known as "Big X." He has organized teams of prisoners to build three tunnels, which he has named Tom, Dick, and Harry.

The Germans soon realized the prisoners were digging, and discovered one tunnel—Tom. However, they haven't found Dick or Harry.

Harry was the tunnel chosen for the escape. It stretches over 100 yards under the camp. Its entrance is hidden under the stove in one of the huts in which the prisoners sleep—hut 104.

The tunnelers have had to dig deep to avoid sound-detecting machines the Germans have rigged up around the compound. They had to use wooden supports to keep the tunnels from collapsing. The wood came from the boards of the prisoners' bunk beds. They used 4,000 boards, and by the time they had finished, no one was getting a good night's sleep.

The tunnels needed air pipes so that those crawling through them wouldn't suffocate. So, the tunnelers joined empty milk powder cans together to make pipes.

The tunnelers dug for up to six hours at a time. At first, they worked in their undershirts and long johns, but in the damp tunnel, their clothes got wet and smelly. In the end, they decided it was easier to wear nothing at all.

HITCHES

One of the prisoners explains to you that the biggest problem they had was getting rid of all the sand that was dug out as the tunnels were built. The Germans had discovered earlier tunnels had been built by spotting the white sand on the blackish gray earth in the camp compound. This time, there were 250 tons of sand to hide.

Finally, the planners came up with a great method that got rid of almost half the sand. Men known as "penguins" stuck one-and-a-half-foot long, sausage-shaped bags made out of towels down each of their trouser legs. The bags were filled with sand and were held by a sort of sling around the prisoner's neck.

The prisoner—often wearing a coat to hide the bulky bags—would then walk over to another prisoner who was working in the camp garden. He would stand in the dirt and release the sand. Then the gardener would quickly cover the white sand with soil.

NERVES

Now that the night of the escape has come and the plan is under way, the prisoners are tense and nervous. They feel that time is

against them. It's the coldest March in 30 years, and the trapdoor at the far end of the tunnel has iced up, slowing things down.

They dig the last two feet to the surface, but find they are about 10 feet away from the edge of the forest. There's a real danger that men will be spotted running across the open ground to the trees. Then, someone has a good idea. They rig up a rope that stretches from behind a bush into the tunnel. One prisoner hides behind the bush. He can see the German sentries on guard. He will give one tug on the rope when it's OK for the next prisoner to run from the tunnel to the forest. Two tugs means to stay put inside.

Some men are panicking in the tunnel because of the long wait. One knocks out a wooden support with his suitcase by mistake and lots of sand falls down. Then, the lights in the tunnel suddenly go out, so it's pitch black.

Despite all these hitches, however, you count 76 men escaping through the tunnel and beginning their long journey to freedom. You wish them luck as they scatter in all directions into the dark night. Then you press EJECT.

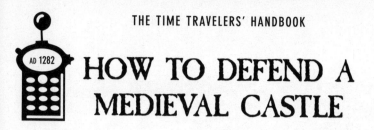

HOW TO DEFEND A MEDIEVAL CASTLE

You land with a jolt to find yourself balancing precariously on the high wall of Hawarden Castle in Wales. A soldier pulls you down from the wall, but as you start to thank him, you see a pretty scary sight. The castle, which stands on top of a hill, is under siege. The sword-wielding army of a Welsh prince named Dafydd ap Gruffudd ap Llywelyn has surrounded the castle and is attacking relentlessly.

The soldier who grabbed you tells you that he and his fellow soldiers have been fighting the Welsh for many years—since 1067, in fact. They built castles along the border with Wales, but failed to completely conquer the Welsh. The mountainous, rugged terrain of Wales and the fierce fighting of the Welsh denied them victory.

THE CALL TO ARMS

It's only recently, in 1277 under the rule of King Edward I, that the conquest of Wales was completed. To cement his victory and maintain control of the land, Edward has built several massive stone castles, including this one. Unfortunately, the Welsh are still angry and keep revolting against the invaders. This is their strongest revolt yet.

The soldier thrusts a crossbow into your hands and tells you to prepare for battle. To your left and right are men armed with bows and arrows, crossbows, or leather pouches filled with stones.

As the attacking army advances up the hill, the soldier quickly shows you how to use the shape of the wall to your advantage.

The wall has been built with a series of square holes cut into the top of it called crenellations. The English soldiers can shoot their arrows through these holes, and then retreat behind the cover of the wall. In the walls of the towers, there are also thin windows known as arrow loops, which are just the right size to shoot arrows through, but very difficult for the attackers down below to aim at.

In between firing arrows, the soldier tells you that this attack has been going on for many days. Roger of Clifford holds this castle and the surrounding settlements for the king. He has retreated with his family and servants into the keep—that is, the inner part of the castle behind you and the strong castle walls.

The keep is the safest place to be. Inside the keep there is enough food, water, and provisions stored to keep people going for weeks.

Your friend praises the great work you're doing with the crossbow, but points out that the Welsh army is coming up the hill toward the castle's battlements with a nasty-looking battering ram. They plan to break down the heavy wooden gates. You look worried, but he doesn't seem too concerned. He points to the battlements above the gatehouse, where an enormous cauldron of water is being heated over a fire. In the floor beneath are the delightfully named "murder holes," through which the cauldron will be emptied. As soon as the attackers get too close, they are going to get a very nasty scalding.

Next, however, the Welsh army starts using massive catapults, called trebuchets, to launch boulders at the outer walls. Soon, you see enemy soldiers swarming into the castle through the huge holes that the boulders have made. You decide it's all getting a bit too close for comfort, and as an arrow whizzes past your ear, you decide it's time to hit EJECT and head home.

HOW TO MAKE A MEDIEVAL HELMET

You can make your own medieval helmet. Then, you will have it ready the next time you are under siege.

You will need:

- a large piece of silver cardstock • scissors • tape
- a pencil • a ruler • some string • a glass jam jar

1. Measure around your head using the piece of string. To do this, hold your string at one end against your forehead one inch above your eyebrows, and wrap the rest of it around your head until the length of the string touches the end. Hold on to the string at the point where it meets the loose end and measure from that point to the end using your ruler. Make a note of the length of the string.

2. Take your cardstock and lay it down lengthwise in front of you, silver-side down. Measure from the left edge of your cardstock the length you noted down and mark it clearly.

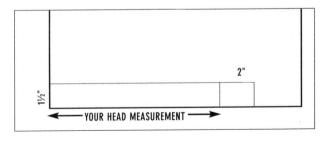

3. Measure and mark 1$^1/_2$ inches up from the edge of the card nearest you. Use this mark to draw a rectangle 1$^1/_2$ inches by the length of your string. Add an extra 2 inches to the right of your rectangle. This will be used to fasten your helmet.

4. Measure and mark 10 inches up from the 1¹/₂ inch line. Divide this up into five equal rectangles (ignoring the 2 inch fastener).

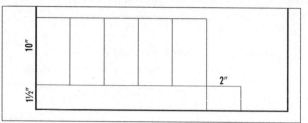

5. Next, take your ruler and place it along the line you have drawn farthest from the bottom of your card. Measure and mark the midpoint of each of the five rectangles.

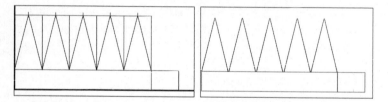

6. Now, use your ruler to draw lines linking the corners of each rectangle along the 1¹/₂ inch line up to the midpoints of the rectangles along the 10 inch line. This will give you five triangle shapes. Cut out your helmet as shown above, putting your leftover card to one side for later.

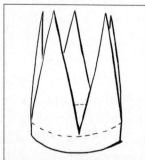

7. Next, roll your cutout into a tall crown shape, silver-side out.

8. Use the 2 inch tab to fasten your helmet by making sure it overlaps fully. Secure this with tape.

9. Take your jam jar and place it open-side down onto the plain side of your leftover card. Draw around it using a pencil and cut out the circle.

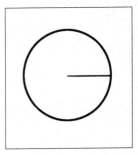

10. Mark the midpoint of your circle and then cut a single line from the edge of the circle to the midpoint. Bend your circle of card into a cone shape and secure this with tape.

11. Take some leftover card and draw a rectangle measuring 8 inches by 2 inches and cut it out. This will be your nose piece.

12. Take your helmet and carefully bend in the triangles until they meet in the middle to make a tall dome shape. Stick these together using tape. Don't worry if this looks messy— you won't be able to see this when you've finished.

13. Use more tape to stick your cone shape to the top of your helmet. It should cover up the joined tops of your triangles and make your helmet more secure.

14. Your helmet is almost finished. Take the nose piece and bend it in half lengthwise so that the two plain edges meet. Unfold it again. This should have made a ridge down the middle. Tape this to the inside of your helmet.

AD 1599

HOW TO ACT IN A SHAKESPEAREAN PLAY

In front of you appears a man with a pointy beard and a twirly mustache. He is pacing around, tugging at his hair, and muttering to himself. You have landed backstage at the Globe Theatre in London, and this is William Shakespeare, who will become probably the most famous playwright in history.

Right now, however, Shakespeare's in trouble. Halfway through a performance of his new play, one of his actors has rushed offstage. The boy has a green face, he's holding his stomach, and groaning about eating one too many eel pies.

THE SHOW MUST GO ON

Just then, Will spots you and decides you'd be the perfect replacement. Before you know it, he's shoving a script in your hand and giving you a few acting tips:

• Speak up. The audience sitting up in the highest gallery are a long way away. If you breathe in from just above your belly button and fill up with air, your voice will be much stronger and travel much farther without needing to shout.

• Speak clearly. Pronounce your words more precisely than you would normally. If you talk too quickly or slur your words, the audience won't be able to understand you and will get bored.

• Look around. The Globe Theatre is circular and the audience is on three sides of the stage, so you need to move your body so you can be seen by everyone.

If you follow these tips, hopefully, the 3,000-strong audience won't get bored. If they do, watch out. Rowdy Elizabethan audiences will throw things. If you see any food flying through the air—duck, or you could get a rotten turnip in the face.

HOW TO STAGE A FIGHT

William Shakespeare has written plays about love, war, witches, murders, ghosts, and shipwrecks—anything to keep his audience interested. He loves to write about fights. The play is *Macbeth* and has a great fight scene. William quickly tells you how to stage a fight so you can take part in the play onstage right now.

Every single move in a stage fight is planned out and rehearsed over and over again. Read his tips and practice with a friend:

1. Arm yourselves. Remember that the whole point of your stage fight is that neither of you gets hurt. So, choose your weapons carefully. The long cardboard tubes you get in wrapping paper are ideal.

2. Decide why you are fighting. This will provide drama. Perhaps one of you is the king and the other is wanting to steal his throne, or you could be pirates fighting over a pot of gold.

3. Find a good place to rehearse, like a yard or park, then you can start to create your fight.

4. Be entertaining. If you both just go *whack, whack, whack* with the swords, it will be boring. Swing around things. Jump off things. Use props: Maybe one of you can drop his sword and be forced to use something else to fight with. Be inventive.

5. Once you have worked out your moves, rehearse them slowly at first until you are sure you both know them in the right order. Then speed them up, and gradually work the fight up to full speed.

Top Tip: Don't forget the sound effects. Grunts, gasps, and shouts are all good. To make it sound really authentic, say things like "Alack!" or "I'm slain." Dying scenes should be as long and drawn out as possible.

HOW TO FIGHT WITH THE SAMURAI

The two men in front of you are a fierce and terrifying sight, clad in strange armor, with wide helmets, and each holding a long, curved sword. They are samurai, members of a group of ancient Japanese warriors who ruled Japan for 700 years. Samurai warriors are considered to be some of the greatest swordsmen in history. Luckily for you, however, they follow a strict code of honor—and that includes not attacking an unarmed time traveler who is considerably shorter than they are.

Your new samurai friends are also extremely polite. They bow and present their beautiful swords for you to look at. Samurai

swords are called *katana* and can take many months to make. They are formed from steel that is heated and then folded over and over again to make it very strong and flexible. As a result, the swords are very valuable. Swords are given names, such as "billowing waves" and "cherry blossom." The names are inspired by a wavy line called the hamon line on the blade of each sword, caused by the joining of the steel. The swords are very sharp and can slice a man in two so quickly that he will continue to walk for several paces before falling down dead.

The two warriors invite you to watch them practicing their sword skills. They move so fast and nimbly, your eyeballs ache keeping up. The clanging, swishing, slicing sound coming from their swords makes one thing clear: You know whose side you'd want to be on in a battle—theirs.

WARRIOR WAYS

You'd love to stay and watch, but a young samurai who is about your age whisks you away. He is learning a martial art called *kendo*, which means "the way of the sword," but he is late because his partner has not turned up, so you agree to go with him.

You join a group of boys. Each has a bamboo stick, which he holds with both hands. Grabbing a spare stick from the side of the room, you move to a position where you can watch the teacher at the front of the group.

You notice that, unlike a modern classroom, everyone here is very well behaved. This is because the samurai live by a code called *Bushido*—which means "the way of the warrior." They value obedience, self-discipline, and bravery above all things. Your friend tells you that the word *samurai* means "one who serves"—not one who whispers and passes notes at the back of the class.

Kendo is performed with a partner, who is referred to as *motodachi*. The class splits into pairs, so you stand opposite your friend. The first part of the practice involves a special ceremony:

1. Stand opposite your *motodachi*, about nine paces apart. Hold your stick, called *shinai*, on your left-hand side if you are right handed, or on your right-hand side if you are left handed.

2. Lift your *shinai* to hip level, and take three steps toward your partner.

3. On the third step, lift your *shinai* up and forward. Your partner should do exactly the same. Hold your *shinai* so the tips are almost touching.

4. Move your left foot so the heels of both your feet are almost touching.

5. Bend your knees and go into a deep squat, spreading your knees wide apart. This is called *sonkyo*.

6. Stand up.

Unfortunately, your knees make a large cracking sound as you squat and you get the giggles. The teacher looks very angry with you, so perhaps it is time to leave. Press EJECT.

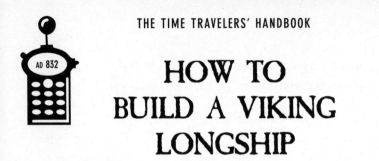

HOW TO BUILD A VIKING LONGSHIP

You've touched down on the coast of Norway during the age of the Vikings. The Vikings are explorers, warriors, and merchants who lived in what is now known as Scandinavia.

You seem to be in a long hut surrounded by several women who are hard at work, sewing together pieces of linen to make a large, square shape. One of them hands you a needle and thread. At that moment, a huge man walks into the hut and saves you from sewing.

The man, who is called Olaf, takes you outside, where dozens of people are busy building a magnificent ship. It is almost ready to set sail. As he walks you around, Olaf tells you exactly what the workers have done so you can try to build your own longship.

Longships can be as long as 100 feet, so you will need to chop down a very tall tree to form the ship's keel—the long central piece that runs all the way along the bottom of the ship. Attach large, curved pieces of wood to each end of the keel to form the front and back of the ship, known as the bow and the stern.

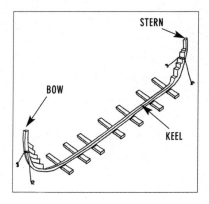

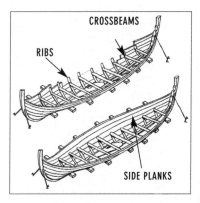

Fix support planks, called ribs and crossbeams, at right angles to the keel. Take some sturdy side planks and attach them from the bow to stern to form the sides and bottom of the ship. Each plank should overlap the one below it and be fixed in place with iron rivets. Add a large block of wood to support the mast.

Lay smooth planks over the crossbeams to form the deck. Fix a large, fish-shaped piece of wood onto the deck for the mast to slip through. This is called the *kløften*. Add trestles, to hold the sail when it is lowered.

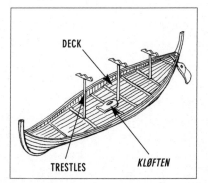

Drill holes in the side of the ship for the long, thin oars to poke through. At the stern of the boat, add a large steering oar. Make sure you make some disks of wood that can fit over the holes to stop water getting in when the oars aren't being used.

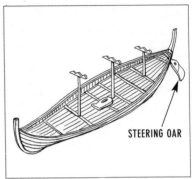

STEERING OAR

To make your ship seaworthy, you need to caulk it. Get some animal fur and dip it into hot tar. The tar is smelly stuff but it will make your ship water-proof. Push your tar-soaked wads of fur between the planks of the ship, making sure there are no gaps.

Olaf tells you he is going to call his ship the *Sea Dragon*. He leads you to a skilled carpenter who is carving a fearsome dragon's head to mount on the bow of the boat.

He invites you to join his voyage, but the deck looks like it will be quite crowded with all those big strong Vikings on board. What's more, pulling the ship's heavy oars doesn't look like fun. So, you wave them off on their way from the shore, and hit the EJECT button.

HOW TO TACKLE A TYRANNOSAURUS REX

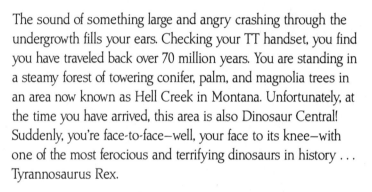

The sound of something large and angry crashing through the undergrowth fills your ears. Checking your TT handset, you find you have traveled back over 70 million years. You are standing in a steamy forest of towering conifer, palm, and magnolia trees in an area now known as Hell Creek in Montana. Unfortunately, at the time you have arrived, this area is also Dinosaur Central! Suddenly, you're face-to-face—well, your face to its knee—with one of the most ferocious and terrifying dinosaurs in history . . . Tyrannosaurus Rex.

DOS AND DON'TS

To minimize your chances of ending up as Tyrannosaurus Rex's lunch, here are some life-saving precautions to take:

- **Don't** try to hide. Tyrannosaurus Rex has very good eyesight and an excellent sense of smell. It will sniff you out very quickly.

- **Do** avoid a Tyrannosaurus Rex's teeth. His powerful jaws are lined with up to 60 of them. Bite marks found on the fossils of other dinosaurs show that Tyrannosaurus Rex can open its massive mouth wide enough to bite off as much as 150 pounds of meat at one time—which is substantially more than the whole of you!

• **Don't** let the Tyrannosaurus Rex step on you. A fully grown Tyrannosaurus Rex is massive–up to 45 feet long, 20 feet tall, and weighing around 8 tons. Even a Tyrannosaurus Rex teenager weighs around 3¹/₂ tons.

• **Don't** be tempted to stand and fight. Even though, compared to its back limbs, a Tyrannosaurus Rex's front limbs are tiny, you wouldn't stand a chance in a boxing match. Its claws pack a powerful punch. Some dinosaur experts think Tyrannosaurus

Rex used its arms for holding struggling prey—and you don't want to prove them right.

• **Do** make a run for it. Tyrannosaurus Rex walks on its two powerful back legs, but can't run very fast. It simply doesn't have the muscle power. Its maximum speed is about 11 miles per hour, and it can't even keep that up for very long.

• **Do** look out for a dinosaur with a mouth like a duck's bill and stay as far away from it as you can. This is an Edmontosaurus, Tyrannosaurus Rex's favorite food.

HOW TO WALK ON THE MOON

No sooner have your feet touched the ground than they leave it again. Somewhat alarmed, you find yourself floating. You're in some kind of spacecraft. You're weightless and confused. Suddenly, you see something outside a window—a huge, round something, a something you've seen almost every night of your life, but never this close—the Moon.

The Moon is so huge and so close, you feel you could almost reach out and touch it. You're on the lunar module *Eagle* that has been launched from the spacecraft *Columbia*. It is a weird-looking contraption—silver, yellow, and orange—with legs, and it is heading for touchdown on the Moon.

On board with you are two astronauts—Neil Armstrong and Buzz Aldrin—and they're about to become the first people to set foot on the Moon.

MOON WALKING FOR BEGINNERS

Walking on the Moon takes a bit of getting used to. Here are some things to watch out for:

• On the Moon, you will weigh six times less than you do on Earth because the force of gravity pulling you toward the Moon's surface is less powerful than the force on Earth.

• It is harder to balance on the Moon, and you will have to lean slightly forward more than usual. When you want to stop, it will take you a few steps to do so.

TOUCHDOWN

You're lucky to be walking on the Moon at all. You and the astronauts had to maneuver around lots of huge boulders and a big crater before you found a landing place.

Buzz enjoys jogging—well, bouncing—on the Moon, but you notice that the moon dust doesn't scatter itself randomly like dust does on Earth. Moon dust travels neatly and precisely so the prints left by his boots are very clear. Because there's no wind, rain, or creatures on the Moon, the footprints will probably still be very clear millions of years from now.

Buzz and Neil struggle to plant the U.S. flag on the Moon's surface. They can't dig its pole very far into the ground, but after some struggling, they coax it upright.

BACK ON BOARD *COLUMBIA*

In the weightless conditions back on *Columbia*, you have time to find out a few things about life in space.

• Eating is tricky. You have to strap your meal tray to one of your legs when you eat. The things on the tray have rubber grips to keep them from floating off. The food comes in little vacuum packs, but once you open a pack, you have to grab hold of the food with your hand quickly, or jab a fork into it to stop it from escaping. You have to suck your drinks out of a tube.

• One of the astronauts warns you to strap yourself to the toilet seat, but he doesn't warn you about the noise the toilet makes. It's the waste being sucked away to somewhere where it won't float back in again.

• Floating about, turning somersaults, and doing backflips inside the spacecraft is lots of fun, but being sick in weightless conditions is not.

• When you take a space nap, you have to tie yourself down first. There's a lot of highly sensitive equipment around, and one bad dream and one flailing arm in the wrong place could wreck the whole space mission.

HOW TO GRADUATE FROM GLADIATOR SCHOOL

AD 108

It's just after dawn and you've landed at the training ground of an Ancient Roman gladiator school. It's called a *ludus* and is full of sweating, grunting men wearing heavy armor warming up for a hard day's training.

As you watch, you don't notice an older man approaching. Thinking you are a slave, he gives you a clip on the ear and tells you to get on with your work. He is called Ferox, and he is a *magister* or trainer at the school. Quickly, you explain to him that you want to become a gladiator. "It's a tough life," Ferox laughs. "And I should know, I was a famous gladiator, myself."

SLAVES AND CRIMINALS

Most of the gladiators in the *ludus* aren't volunteers. Most of the men and women here are slaves or criminals, others are prisoners of war. They didn't choose to be here, and they can't choose to leave. Gladiators only gain their freedom if they manage to survive several years of fighting.

It's not all bad. At the *ludus*, the gladiators are looked after well, and given food and medical treatment when they need it. They are very competitive and strive to work their way up grades called *paloi* to become the *primus palus*—the best and most respected gladiator in the *ludus*. A *primus palus* can become as famous as a Superbowl quarterback is today.

IN THE ARENA

Today, there is going to be a big gladiatorial contest in the arena, and Ferox says you can come along to help. As you enter the arena, the roar of 50,000 spectators almost shatters your eardrums. The organizer of the contest smiles and waves at the crowd from his chariot, which is part of the parade. Behind him come the gladiators and the slaves who carry their armor, and then you. The man whose armor you are carrying used to be a soldier, but he was captured during a battle. For three years, he has fought as a gladiator, and today is his last contest. If he survives, he'll be free.

You follow your gladiator down a passage to a room beneath the arena. It's a dark, terrifying place down here. You hear the crowd above baying for blood. Your gladiator has chosen a curved sword, a shield, leg armor, and a helmet. He prefers to dress lightly so he can move around more easily.

Suddenly, a trapdoor opens above you. You hear the roar of the crowd get louder. Your gladiator's last fight is going to be against what looks like a very fierce-looking gladiator who hasn't lost a fight yet. You hit EJECT—things are about to get messy.

PLAY *PRIMUS PALUS*

Back in the future, it's a good idea to stay in fighting shape in case you land back in the arena when you least expect it. Find an open space, like a large yard or park, set up this four-station obstacle course, and train with your friends. Who will be *primus palus*—the greatest gladiator of all?

You will need:
• at least two players • a large old bedsheet (one that can get muddy without anyone getting angry) • large stones
• six empty cereal boxes • a tennis ball • a tablespoon
• a bucket • a beanbag • a stopwatch

Obstacle One. Spread out your sheet and place large stones on each corner to anchor it down. Put more along two opposite sides to hold it down, leaving enough slack for gladiators to crawl on their stomachs beneath it. The first one to the other end wins.

Obstacle Two. Stand the six cereal boxes in a straight line about 20 inches apart. If it is a windy day, fill the boxes with stones. This standing jump sequence is designed to strengthen your legs and improve balance. Competitors need to jump with both feet together over each box without taking an extra step or knocking the boxes over. If they do, they have to start again at the beginning.

Obstacle Three. Place the spoon and tennis ball on the ground and the bucket 11 yards away from them. This obstacle is a test of both coordination and instinct. Walk as fast as you can toward the bucket, balancing the tennis ball on the spoon. If you drop the ball, you need to start again. When you reach the bucket, turn around so your back is to the bucket, and attempt to throw the ball over your head and into the bucket using the spoon.

Obstacle Four. Place the beanbag next to the bucket used in Obstacle Three. When a gladiator has successfully thrown the ball into the bucket, he must balance the beanbag on top of his head and run backward along the length of the course to the start without dropping it.

AND THE WINNER IS . . .

Once you have set up your course and each of the players understands what to do at the various obstacles, the game can begin. Take turns completing the course, one at a time. Practice a few times to work out your tactics. Then, when everyone is ready, take your stopwatch and time each gladiator completing the course. The fastest is the winner and takes the title *primus palus*.

Top Tip: Every gladiator has different strengths. Time each event separately to find out who is the best at each one.

HOW TO PUT OUT THE GREAT FIRE OF LONDON

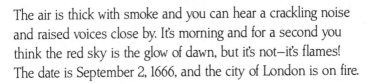

The air is thick with smoke and you can hear a crackling noise and raised voices close by. It's morning and for a second you think the red sky is the glow of dawn, but it's not—it's flames! The date is September 2, 1666, and the city of London is on fire.

A man shoves a long iron pole with a hook on the end into your hands and orders you to follow him. There's no time for introductions as you're about to join one of the teams of people fighting desperately to stop the fire before it destroys the whole city.

FIGHTING FIRE

Ahead, you see people using axes, ropes, and hooks to pull down a row of houses. They are attempting to make a big enough gap in the buildings that the fire can't leap across it. It's tough work and as the fire gets closer, you can feel the intense heat.

The plan isn't working, and the fire is jumping the gaps as quickly as they are created. You suggest calling the fire department, but everyone just looks at you as if you are mad. In 1666, there is no fire department. Each neighborhood has some basic equipment to stop fires, such as leather buckets for water, as well as axes, hooks, and ladders. There is even something called a fire squirt that pumps water, but against this blaze, it is about as much use as a giant water pistol.

FEAR FIGHTING

Rumor has it that the fire started this morning at a bakery in Pudding Lane. London at this time is full of wooden houses all crammed together, so the fire is spreading quickly, leaping from building to building, destroying everything in its path. To make things worse, there are lots of storehouses in the area filled with oil, pitch, and tar—all of which catch fire very easily.

The man tells you that people have been slow to realize how bad the fire is. They're refusing to let their homes be pulled down because of the cost of rebuilding them.

You stick around to help out and by the end of the second day, you see lots of Londoners forced to leave their homes. Thieves and looters use this as an opportunity to help themselves to things in abandoned houses. Many owners of carts and riverboats also take advantage of people trying to escape the fire by charging huge amounts to carry them to safety.

Soldiers and sailors have to be called in to help. They use gunpowder to blast rows of houses out of the way to stop the fire spreading. Eventually, this begins to work, and after four days, the fire is finally put out. Though huge areas of the city have been leveled by the fire, amazingly it is reported that only eight people died in the blaze. You wonder how this can be possible with London seeming to be so crowded, and the speed at which the fire spread. Now the cleanup can begin, but this doesn't look quite as exciting as fighting the fire, so you decide to hit EJECT.

WARNING

Fighting fires in the present is something best left to the professionals, but if you do discover a fire, leave the area immediately and contact the Fire Department.

Never attempt to fight the fire yourself.

HOW TO LEAP A MINOAN BULL

It's hot, there's a sparkly sea, olive trees, and green hills—and you realize you have landed on the beautiful island of Crete, the largest of the Greek Islands. What you don't know is that you are about to witness one of the most spectacular and dangerous sports of all time. It is a sport that tests not only a man's strength, speed, and agility, but also his courage (or stupidity, depending on how you look at it).

A boy wearing a tunic approaches and asks if you'd like to follow him. He is a Minoan, a member of the great civilization that live on Crete and on islands all around the Aegean Sea in 1500 BC.

He leads you to the edge of a field where you see an enormous, angry bull scratching at the ground with one of its hooves. In front of it stands a young man who seems to be taunting it, wanting the bull to charge at him. The man is known as a leaper and what he wants to do is leap over the bull in a sport that is part dance, part acrobatics, and totally crazy.

THE BULL LEAPER

You watch the bull lunge toward the leaper. Amazingly, instead of running away, the young man stands still. As the bull reaches him, the leaper reaches out and grabs its horns. Immediately, the bull tosses back his head, throwing the man into the air and over his back. The leaper then lets go of the horns and lands expertly on both feet on top of the bull's back. From here, he leaps into the air, performing a perfect somersault, and lands safely behind the bull.

Bulls are very important to the Minoan people. The people are called Minoan after a king from long ago named Minos. Legend has it that King Minos built a huge maze to contain a monster that was half man and half bull. This monster was called the Minotaur.

The Minotaur terrorized the island and had to be fed with human flesh until it was eventually killed by a brave hero from Athens named Theseus.

MEGA MISTAKE

As you watch the leaper, you begin to appreciate the beauty of the sport. It's graceful and gymnastic, and the leapers seem extremely brave. Perhaps you have been watching for too long, because one of the leapers asks you if you would like a turn. Before you know it, you are face-to-face with the biggest and angriest bull of all. Having been leapt over so many times, he looks ready to trample someone.

As the bull is thundering closer and closer, you decide this is not the time to try a new sport, and that it would make sense to go back to the future and get some practice first. So, just as you can feel the bull's breath on your cheek, you hit EJECT.

HOW TO PLAY LEAPING BULLS

To practice your bull-leaping skills in a park or yard, you will need two teams. The following instructions are for teams with three members, but the more the merrier.

Measure out a course 25 yards long, with a clearly marked start and finish line. (The course will need to be longer if you have more than three people in a team.)

Each team has one leaper and the rest of its members are bulls. The bulls in each team line up along the length of the course, Team A standing 5 yards away from Team B. The first bull in each team stands about 4 yards from the starting line and the second bull stands 4 yards farther along the course and so on.

All the bulls must stand sideways to the finish line. They bend over, putting their elbows on their thighs, and tucking their heads into their chests with their index fingers pointing upward either side of their head. These are the bulls' horns.

The two leapers stand on the starting line. When the game begins, the leapers run toward the first bull in their line. They place their hands in the center of the bull's back and leap over. They repeat this over each of the bulls until they have leapt the last one. The leapers then bend over to become bulls themselves and the first bull in the row becomes the leaper.

Continue until the first leaper has leapt twice then sprinted to the finish line. The first team with a leaper over the line wins.

WARNING

Leaping real bulls is something that should be left in the past. Time travelers should never attempt to leap a bull. You could get yourself badly injured or killed.

HOW TO MAKE AN EGYPTIAN MUMMY

The room you've just landed in has two people in it, but only one of them is alive—fortunately, that's you. The other person is a man lying flat out on a stone slab, looking very, very dead.

Your head is buzzing with questions—who is he, what's he doing there, and, most of all, should you hit EJECT and head home? Just then, a man comes in and he has all the answers. He explains that you've landed in the workshop of an Ancient Egyptian embalmer. He is the chief embalmer, and he invites you to stay and help.

His job is making the bodies of dead rich people into mummies, so that they don't rot away inside their tombs. He and his team are about to get started on this one.

EMBALMING

A word of warning here: Making an Egyptian mummy is not just about wrapping a few bandages around a dead body. A lot of grisly stuff goes on first. So, if you're the sort who feels a bit queasy seeing one tiny drop of blood, you'd better toughen up— and fast—or hit EJECT. You decide to stay and the embalmer starts to give you instructions.

1. Push a long hook up the dead man's nose. This breaks up his brain so that you can pull it out through his nose.

2. Make a slit in the side of the body and pull out the dead man's internal organs. The embalmer asks if you are sure that you want to do this. Top time travelers are always open to new experiences, so you do—but wish you hadn't. Intestines are long, slimy, stinky and make a lot of squelching noises on their way out.

3. Place the different organs in separate jars called canopic jars—one for the lungs, the liver, the stomach, and the intestines.

The embalmer tells you to leave the heart in the body because the dead person needs it in the next world.

4. Now, cover the whole body with special salt called natron. Stuff small packets of natron inside the body. It will dry the body out, preserve it, and cut down on smells, too.

5. The chief embalmer tells you that the body must now be left covered in the natron for around 40 days, until it is completely dried out. After that time, it will look much thinner and darker. The embalmers will then stuff the body to make it a normal shape again, and sew up the slit you made in the side of the body. It's now ready for wrapping.

GET WRAPPING

The workshop contains bodies that are at various stages of the mummification process. So now, you are told to get to work wrapping a body that was embalmed 40 days earlier. The chief embalmer tells you it's precise, painstaking work. It must be done extremely neatly, because the dead man you are wrapping has a rich and powerful family who are very fussy.

You start by helping to crisscross bandages across the body, starting with the head and then individually wrapping the fingers

and toes. The bandages are wrapped in layers, and some of them are decorated with prayers. You're as careful as you can be, but it's tricky work and you get a little confused, so they decide to give you the job of sprinkling incense instead.

You sprinkle strong-smelling incense, such as frankincense and myrrh, between each layer of bandages. You place pieces of jewelry, called amulets, between the layers to ward off evil.

JOURNEY TO THE UNDERWORLD

While they bandage, the embalmers explain that they believe the dead man's spirit is about to go on a long journey through the underworld. At the end of it, he'll meet Osiris, who is the lord of the underworld. If Osiris thinks the man has been good, his spirit will be reunited with his body and he'll live in the afterlife.

People believe that the afterlife will be a better version of the world they live in now. So, the dead man's family and friends do all they can to help him on his journey. They write messages and inscriptions on his coffin, and put lots of things in the tomb they think he might need in the afterlife, such as food, clothes, furniture, and even underwear. They put small figurines of his servants in his tomb—these are called *Ushabtis*. They put the Book of the Dead in too, which is sort of a travel guide to the afterlife.

Finally, the chief embalmer puts a mask over the mummy's face. And, because it's hard to tell who's who when they're covered head to foot in bandages, he attaches a label saying who is inside. He doesn't want the mummy to go off to the wrong funeral.

Now, you are finished, and it's time to get away from the stinky workshop, so you hit EJECT.

HOW TO MAKE A FLINT AXE

Suddenly, you hear the sounds of two stones being struck together behind you. You spin around and see a man sitting on the ground. He is chipping away at a large hunk of rock with a smaller rock.

He is making an axe, but when it is finished, it doesn't look like any axe you've seen before. It doesn't even have a handle. He sees you are puzzled and walks toward a small sapling. Holding the axe in the palm of his hand, blade-side out, he hits the sapling at the base. It comes down in one stroke. He picks it up and then uses the edge of the blade to scrape off some bark at the base. He pulls on the bark and it comes off in one long strip, which he says can be used for string or for weaving baskets.

He hands you a chunk of rock that he says is flint, and tells you to try.

STONE AGE STEP-BY-STEP

You will need:

• a large piece of dark quartz • protective glasses • a few pebbles of different shapes and sizes • a piece of bone or hard wood • a thick leather cloth or a doubled-up towel

1. First, select the piece of quartz you will be shaping. If possible, get a piece that is already a flattish round or oval shape. If you tap the quartz, and it makes a muffled sound, this means there is a fault inside which will make it weak and difficult to knap, or shape into a stone tool.

2. Rest your piece of quartz on a thick leather cloth (or towel) on your left knee and steady it with your left hand if you are right handed (the other way if you are left handed).

3. Use one of your pebbles to strike the longest side of the quartz. Make blows on one side rather than hitting it in the middle. This will make sure you remove some long shards from the edge of the quartz, making it more pointed.

4. As you knap, don't throw away the flakes that chip off. They can be made into arrowheads and small tools for scraping the flesh away from an animal skin. Be careful, they are very sharp.

5. Once you have shaped your big piece of quartz so that it looks narrower on one side than the other (this is the chopping side of the axe), you are ready to start making a sharp edge.

6. With a smaller pebble, continue flaking off long pieces of quartz in the same way as you did before—but this time, use less force, and be especially careful to knap along the long face of the axe.

As the edge of the axe gets thinner, you'll need to use your pieces of bone or wood instead of the pebble to avoid breaking off too much quartz at one time.

7. Place the axe on a hard surface, and with the chopping side closest to the surface, grind the pointed end of your piece of wood in a twisting motion against the edge of the axe. This will allow you to take off tiny pieces of quartz until your axe is the perfect shape.

WARNING

Shards of quartz can be as sharp as kitchen knives. Wear protective glasses and be sure to cover your lap. Be very careful when getting rid of the shards. Wrap them in several sheets of newspaper and throw them in the trash.

Never knap quartz indoors because rock dust can be very bad for your lungs.

HOW TO SURVIVE THE BLITZ IN BRITAIN

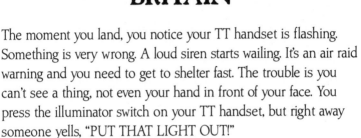

The moment you land, you notice your TT handset is flashing. Something is very wrong. A loud siren starts wailing. It's an air raid warning and you need to get to shelter fast. The trouble is you can't see a thing, not even your hand in front of your face. You press the illuminator switch on your TT handset, but right away someone yells, "PUT THAT LIGHT OUT!"

It's 1940, and you've landed in the middle of the Blitz. The Blitz is the name people are giving to a period during World War II when, night after night, German planes dropped bombs on cities all over Britain.

THE BLACKOUT

The siren is still blaring and you hear the whistling noise of a bomb dropping to the ground. There is a flash of light and the deafening sound of the explosion. A woman grabs your hand, and pulls you through a door and down some steps. There is light down here and you can see where you are. You're in a London subway station packed with people sheltering from a nighttime bombing raid on the city.

The lady who grabbed you is called Sylvia. Her husband is away fighting. She apologizes for shouting at you, but warns you that you can get in a lot of trouble for showing a light during a blackout. During a blackout, everyone has to cover up his windows with thick black curtains. The street lamps are shaded so they let out only a tiny bit of light, and even car headlights are positioned to point downward and shine through black slits. The government hopes the darkness will make it impossible for the pilots of German bombers to target Britain's cities from the air.

GOING UNDERGROUND

The station is dirty with mice scrambling around. It smells because the toilets are closed and people are having to use buckets, instead. But it is the safest place to be. Sylvia explains that at the beginning of the war, the government banned people from sheltering down here. So, she would just buy a ticket to travel on the subway, and only come up when the all-clear sirens sounded to tell people the bombers had gone. Now more than 200,000 people take cover in stations all over London. There are public

shelters, but not enough for everyone, and Sylvia doesn't have a yard in which to build a homemade shelter called an Anderson shelter.

Aboveground, you can still hear the bombs exploding and every so often, the bench you are sitting on shakes. Sylvia is worried about what she will find when the air raid ends. Last week, one family on her street returned from the shelter to find a heap of rubble where their house used to be.

BOMBS IN THE BLITZ

Sylvia tells you the German planes overhead are dropping two kinds of bombs:

1. Fire bombs, known as incendiary bombs. The Germans drop these first, in clusters. The bombs are small, but full of chemicals, and burst into flames wherever they land. They cause lots of damage and create light for the pilots to see where to drop the rest of their bombs.

2. High-explosive bombs—packed with explosives. Most of these explode on impact, destroying the buildings around them.

Others have timers on them and explode hours later, without any warning. Army bomb disposal experts try to disarm them, but it's dangerous work and many are killed.

Sylvia tells you that last week, on November 14, 1940, German bombers dropped around 500 tons of bombs on the city of Coventry near Birmingham, England. This killed 568 people and injured over 1,000. More than 60,000 buildings were destroyed.

BEATING THE BLITZ BLUES

• Bring earplugs. If you thought your dad's snoring was bad, an air raid is much worse. The wail of the sirens, the thump of exploding bombs, and the crashing as buildings collapse is terrifying. To keep everyone's spirits up and drown out the sound of the bombs, why not try singing?

• Bring something to do. During a raid, you can be in the shelter for a long time. Sylvia is knitting, but you could try a board game, or a pack of cards.

• Don't go out after sunset unless you have to. The blackout has caused chaos on the roads. People can't see where they are going. They bump into lampposts, fall off bridges, and cars have crashed into canals.

• Bring a snack. Sadly, food is in short supply. The government controls how much food people can have—this is called rationing.

• Get evacuated—lots of children have been sent to the countryside to live with families away from the bombs (see pages 19 to 21). Sylvia has two daughters who have been evacuated to Wales.

HOW NOT TO SINK WITH THE *TITANIC*

AD 1912

You've landed on RMS *Titanic*–the biggest passenger steamship in the world. The *Titanic* is sailing about 400 miles off the coast of Newfoundland on its first voyage across the Atlantic Ocean from Southampton, England, to New York City. You're standing at the top of the Grand Staircase. It's huge, and sweeps down five decks of the ship in a long curve. It's just too tempting. You hop on the banister and slide down to the first-class dining room below. You've only been on this ship for 20 minutes and you've already found a swimming pool, a gym, a squash court, and even a library. It's like a luxurious floating palace–on the top decks, anyway.

At the bottom of the staircase, there is a restaurant full of well-dressed people.

The ladies are dripping with diamonds that glitter almost as much as the chandeliers that hang from the ceiling above their heads. The food looks delicious, too.

TEMPTING FATE

Feeling a little hungry, you sit down, hoping to get some food. The people at your table are impressed with the ship, too. "RMS *Titanic* is the first unsinkable ship ever built," enthuses one man. You want to say something—if there's one thing you know about the *Titanic* it's that it is far from unsinkable. Remember—you must never change the course of history (see page 3). In a few hours, RMS *Titanic* will be at the bottom of the ocean. More than 2,200 people are on board, 1,517 of them will die, and there is nothing you can do about it.

THAT SINKING FEELING

A waiter notices you, and looks as if he's about to ask whether you belong in first class. So, you shoot out onto the deck. An icy wind cuts straight through you, and even though it's dark outside, you see a faint white shape looming in the distance . . . an iceberg.

Unable to stop yourself, you run to tell a member of the crew. He has already seen it—but it's too late. "It doesn't look too big," says the crewman, but you know that only about one ninth of an iceberg can be seen from the surface. It is what is under water that can do the damage. You persuade him to sound the alarm. The crew have already had warnings from other ships in the area, but they have ignored them.

There is the terrible sound of ripping metal as this gigantic ship hits the iceberg. It tears holes all the way along its side below the

waterline and water rushes into the hull. The whole deck shudders, but the crewman tells you not to worry—the *Titanic* is unsinkable.

You look back into the dining room, where the music is still playing and food is still being served, and people look as if nothing is happening. They laugh at the few passengers who have gone to fetch life jackets. They really don't think the ship will sink.

TITANIC SURVIVAL TIPS

As a time traveler, you know you can't do anything to save anyone else on board. You can and you must save yourself.

- Get to a lifeboat fast—there aren't enough for all the people on board. The company who built the ship recommended it should have 48 lifeboats to hold all the passengers, but the White Star Line, who owns the *Titanic*, only put on 20. There are 16 wooden boats that hold 65 passengers, and 4 collapsible boats that hold 47. They aren't even completely filling the ones they have launched—one boat leaves with only 12 people on board.

- Tell the crewmen in charge of the lifeboats how old you are. Women and children are allowed to board the lifeboats first.

- Act wealthy. Almost all the women and children in first class survive (first class is for the richest passengers), as do most in second. Fewer than half the women and children in third class survive. Most people in third class have not been told where the lifeboats are anyway and can't get up to the higher decks.

- Stay in the lifeboat. The sea is freezing. Some people will survive the actual sinking of the ship, but few will last long in the freezing water.

HOW TO SURVIVE A VIKING RAID

AD 839

"Save yourselves, the Vikings are coming!" A cry pierces the morning air as you tumble into the long grass beside a stone wall. You find yourself in a tiny walled settlement beside a monastery on the coast of Ireland. It's a beautiful spot, if it wasn't for the six Viking longships that have just appeared on the horizon.

The monks and villagers are panicking. They must try to hide the monastery's treasures and get as many people as possible to safety before the ruthless raiders get to shore.

BURIED TREASURE

A monk hurrying past you thrusts a golden goblet covered in rubies and emeralds into your hands. "Follow me!" he shouts, and takes you through the monastery to a spot under a tree beside the walls. There, you see a freshly dug hole that the other monks

are filling with armfuls of gold coins, religious books, and silver cups and plates.

The monks hope that by burying their treasure, they can stop it from falling into the hands of the raiders, who have come to steal it.

In the distance, you can see that the Vikings have landed on shore. Their longships are designed to sail up shallow rivers and to land on the shores of sandy beaches, making it easy for the men on board to get ashore quickly. Some raiders are on horseback. Planks are pushed out from the ships, and the horses walk on them down to the beach. Other raiders are on foot, shrieking and shouting, as they run toward the settlement. Only a small group of men are left behind to guard the ships.

You spot a group of Vikings killing a herdsman who had been grazing his sheep on the hills above the beach. They herd the sheep back toward their boats and will enjoy eating them later to celebrate the spoils of their raid.

THE ENEMY AT THE GATES

A terrible noise reaches your ears. Raiders are using a battering ram to break down the wooden gate to the monastery. As the gate splinters and falls, men wearing helmets that flash in the morning sun pour in through the gap. Mercilessly, they cut down monks and villagers with their big metal swords. Some raiders set fire to the houses, once they have searched them for anything worth stealing.

The abbot, who is in charge of the monastery, pulls you and another monk to one side and tells you to go for help at the fort a half mile away.

As quickly as you can, you help each other over the wall at the back of the monastery garden. As you look back, you can see a long line of women and children who have been rounded up and are being led toward the longships. The Vikings will take them back to Norway, in Scandinavia, and sell them as slaves. You can also see that they have taken the abbot who sent you for help. He will be held for ransom—the church will need to pay a fortune in gold to have him returned safely.

The raiders know they don't have long before help arrives, so they are carrying off anything of any value as quickly as they can. The settlement disappears from view as you run toward the fort. All you can see is a plume of smoke rising from the burning buildings. You wonder if the Vikings have found the hidden treasure beside the wall. If not, it might be worth looking for it when you go back to the future. It might still be buried there and the local museum would love to have the treasure on display for visitors.

As you reach the fort, you send the monk ahead to plead for help. You have seen enough, and since there is nothing you can do, it is time to go.

HOW TO WRITE IN HIEROGLYPHS

You land in what looks like a temple, in front of tall sandstone walls that are engraved with lots of pictures. The pictures, which run up and down the walls in straight lines, are hieroglyphs–one of the very first forms of writing.

You spend a moment trying to work out what all the pictures mean, but even though you recognize some of the shapes– such as birds and snakes–you can't make heads or tails of it.

PICTURE POWER

You look around for someone who might be able to help and spot a young man with a partly shaven head walking up the steps of the temple. He has a number of papyrus scrolls (see pages 17 to 18) under his arm. Politely, you ask him to help you understand what the hieroglyphs mean. His name is Suten Anu. He is a scribe at the palace of the pharaoh, the king of Egypt.

Suten tells you that the writing you see on the walls was taught to Egyptians by Thoth, the god of wisdom. Suten believes that the pictures have a power all of their own. It would take years to teach you how to read all of the symbols—there are over 700 of them—but he is happy to give you a few pointers.

SOUNDS LIKE . . .

Suten Anu unrolls one of his papyrus scrolls that contains a list of the symbols most commonly used in the writing. He explains that all of them stand for sounds. He says each sound as he runs his finger down the list.

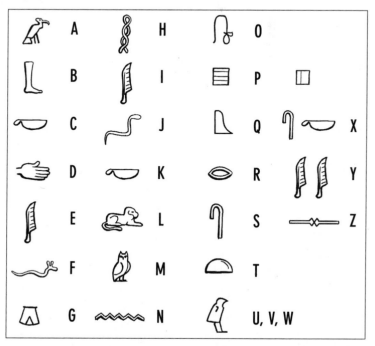

He indicates matching pictures on the walls and points out the little strokes that appear underneath some of them. He says if you see a stroke under a sound symbol, it means the symbol also stands for an object. For example:

You notice that aren't any punctuation marks, such as periods or question marks, on his list of symbols. Suten looks at you blankly, and you guess they don't have any.

To make things more confusing, the hieroglyphs can be drawn left to right or right to left, whichever fits the space best.

CARTOUCHE FOR A KING OR QUEEN

Some hieroglyphs are written in oval frames. These are special ones, known as cartouches. They contain the names of kings and queens. People believe the oval frame protects the royal name.

You ask Suten if he could show you how to write your own name in hieroglyphs. He suggests you start by spelling it out with the sound hieroglyphs he showed you earlier, matching the sounds to the letters in your name. Then you attempt to write his name.

He laughs—it is not quite how he would do it, but he thinks that with practice, you could make a very good scribe.

MAKE A CARTOUCHE

Why not practice your hieroglyphic writing by making a cartouche of your own name?

You will need:

• a sheet of paper and a pencil • self-hardening modeling clay
• a dinner knife • a rolling pin • a thin knitting needle or skewer
• some paint • paintbrushes • glue

1. Plan your cartouche on paper first. Use the list on page 93 to pick out all the letters in your name and write them out on a piece of paper.

2. Roll out your clay with a rolling pin, until it is ½ inch thick.

3. Cut out an oval shape using a dinner knife. (You can make your cartouche any size you like, but 10 inches by 5 inches should fit most names well.)

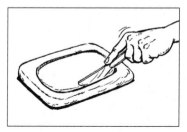

4. Make the rest of your clay into a long sausage shape by rolling it between your palms. It needs to be long enough so you can attach it all the way around the edge of the oval you cut out.

5. Next, carve the hieroglyphs that spell out your name into the clay, using a skewer. Do it lightly first, to check that you can fit your name in. Then, go over your hieroglyphs again, pressing a bit harder.

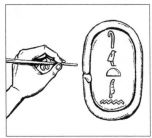

6. When you have finished, let the clay dry, or bake it following the instructions on the package.

7. Paint your cartouche with a coat of yellow paint to make the clay look like sandstone. Then leave it to dry.

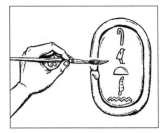

8. When the yellow paint is completely dry, use a thin paintbrush to paint your hieroglyphs in bold colors.

Display your finished cartouche somewhere in your room to alert your family to your royal status. It might make them treat you like a pharaoh, and that is good—pharaohs were treated like gods!

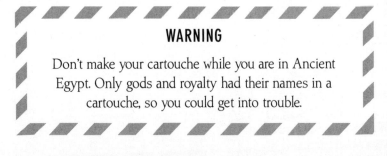

WARNING

Don't make your cartouche while you are in Ancient Egypt. Only gods and royalty had their names in a cartouche, so you could get into trouble.

HOW TO TRAVEL ON THE UNDERGROUND RAILROAD

AD 1850

You are crouched in a small, dark, dusty space, and there's someone beside you–a young man, and he looks terrified. He is hiding from something. Things are not looking good. You have landed in the state of Alabama, and the man beside you, who is called Benjamin, is a slave on the run.

Nearby, you hear loud voices and heavy footsteps. You are about to ask who is out there, but Benjamin motions you to keep quiet. His freedom depends on not being found. So does his life. You hear furniture being moved, doors slamming, and dogs barking in the distance. Then, silence.

Benjamin breathes a deep sigh of relief. He's safe–for now, anyway.

He is hiding from federal marshals, who are the men whose job is to catch Benjamin and send him back to the farm and the miserable life that he has escaped from.

Benjamin is traveling on the Underground Railroad. He tells you that the owner of the building you are hiding in is a "station master." You realize you are squashed into a secret space behind a bookcase. When you come out from behind it, you expect to see a station platform, or at least some train tracks, but you don't. This is because the railroad you are about to travel on is no ordinary railroad.

MAKING TRACKS

Benjamin was born on a farm about 18 miles south of here. As a slave, he was the property of the farmer. This meant he could be bought or sold at any time. Life for slaves on the farm was incredibly hard. Benjamin was beaten if he did not work hard enough and he saw many slaves killed.

Benjamin's parents were slaves, but they weren't born slaves. Many years ago, they were taken by force from Africa by slave traders and brought to America.

ALL ABOARD

• The Underground Railroad isn't a railroad at all. It is the name given to routes that stretch from the south of the United States to the north and into Canada. They are called "underground" because they are secret. Runaway slaves, known as "packages," are helped along the route by organizations of people who work to end slavery.

• Roughly every 12 miles along the Railroad, there are safe places for the runaways to stop, rest, and eat. These places are called "stations."

• The Railroad moves runaways from the southern states of the U.S.A. where keeping slaves is legal, through the northern states, and all the way to freedom in Canada. Because slaves are owned by their masters, it is illegal for them to run away, or for anyone to help them escape. Punishments for doing so are harsh.

• Though the man who runs the safe house you and Benjamin are in today is known as a station master, the people who travel with and guide the runaways between stations are called "conductors."

• Benjamin, and people like him, need all the help they can get. Big rewards are offered to anyone who catches runaways. As a result, not only do federal marshals hunt them—professional bounty hunters and ordinary people are looking for them, too.

MOVING ON

A conductor has arrived to help Benjamin. Her name is Harriet Tubman, otherwise known as General Tubman, or Moses, because of her success at guiding people to freedom. She has helped hundreds of people escape north, so Benjamin is in good hands.

You ask Harriet if you can go along, too. She agrees. First, however, she gives you some stern advice that may save your life.

FOLLOW THE SIGNALS

• **Travel at night.** You will be harder to spot. Look out for the North Star and head toward it. It will guide you north to Canada and to safety.

• **Stay among the trees.** Trees will hide you from view, but they can also help you find your way. Look at their trunks. More moss grows on one side than the other—the side facing north should have more moss.

• **Look out for safe houses.** A lamp hanging from a post outside a house is a sign that it is safe for you to stop there. You will find somewhere to rest and a good meal.

• **Sing along.** Listen to the songs sung by fellow runaways. Some songs contain advice to travelers. One song called "Wade in the Water" advises a traveler to stay close to rivers and wade through them to throw tracker dogs off your scent.

• **Keep moving.** It is legal for slave owners to hunt for their slaves anywhere in the United States. The only safe place is Canada. The Canadian government refuses to send slaves back to their owners. Sadly, Canada is a long way north of Alabama.

HOW TO INVENT WRITING WITH THE SUMERIANS

3100 BC

You've just touched down in Ancient Mesopotamia, an area now known as Iraq. The Sumerians (the name given to the people who lived there in 3100 BC) are a brainy bunch. They are good at building, farming, math, astronomy, and all sorts of other things. They're extremely good at inventing things, too. Some experts think that they may even have invented the wheel, so keep your eyes peeled for proof.

It might not look like it, but the man sitting down right beside you is busy inventing right now. He's writing. Time travelers will tell you that the Sumerians were the first people in the history of the world known to have used writing. This is a truly historical moment, so sit yourself down and join him.

THE WRITE STUFF

Even though the Sumerians are very smart, they haven't invented paper. The man hands you a wet clay tablet to write on. There are no pens or pencils in Mesopotamia either, so he lends you one of his spare writing sticks, called a stylus. It has a pointed end for making marks in the wet clay.

WRITE HERE, WRITE NOW

The man tells you the reason he is writing is because people need a way to keep records of the crops they are growing, and the things they are making. He is using the very earliest form of Sumerian writing, a writing that will change and develop over the next 2,000 years.

He makes the symbol for barley, something Sumerians grow a lot of, by pushing his stylus into the soft clay, and drawing lines, like this:

The finished symbol looks a bit like some of the logos you see around in the present, but not like any word you have seen before. The man draws more picture symbols and asks you to guess what each one means (see the answers on page 117).

WRITER'S BLOCKS

Back in the present, you will find quite a few clay tablets that have survived from Sumerian times—maybe even the one your friend is working on right now. The reason for this is that all the inventing the Sumerians did made them rich. As a result, people who lived around them grew jealous and attacked the Sumerians, attempting to steal from them. One way they would attack was to burn Sumerian buildings. Inside burning buildings, the clay writing tablets got baked hard, and were preserved for centuries.

INVENT YOUR OWN WRITING

Why not try your hand at creating your own Sumerian-style symbols for things around today that you like best?

You will need:
• a pencil • some paper • a sharp stick
• some modeling clay • a rolling pin • an oven

Use the pencil and paper to design some personalized symbols. You can create a symbol for anything—a car, a plane, a skateboard, a pizza, a cell phone, your mother, whatever you like. However, make sure the symbols are simple, so you can copy the shapes into clay.

Next, it's time to make a clay tablet. Take a fist-sized lump of clay and roll it out, using a rolling pin, into a square shape—about a half inch thick. This will be your tablet.

Use the sharp stick (the stylus) to make your symbols in the clay tablet. The best thing about your own Sumerian tablet is that you don't need an attacking army to bake it—just bake it in your oven, following the instructions on the package of modeling clay. Remember, ALWAYS cook with an adult and ask permission to use the oven.

When your clay is baked, carefully remove it from the oven and let it cool. Maybe a kid in 2030 will find it and use his TT handset to come back to visit you to ask what the symbols mean.

HOW TO SURVIVE THE BLACK DEATH

AD 1348

Splat—you've landed in a lumpy substance that smells suspiciously like horse poop, in a filthy street in the middle of Florence, Italy.

The first thing you notice is the smell. In the 21st century, Florence is famed for magnificent art and architecture, but there isn't much evidence of that now. There's just a foul stench and a sense of impending doom. You've arrived when the city is in the grip of the Black Death, a deadly disease that will eventually kill about a third of all the people in Europe.

You have two options—hit the EJECT button and get out of here (it really does smell awful), or stick around to see what's going on.

CAUTION

• The Black Death, otherwise known as the plague, is highly contagious, and can cause a painful death.

• Avoid anyone who looks sick. They may be coughing up blood that contains plague bacteria.

• Avoid rats or anywhere they might be hiding. Rats don't cause the disease, but the fleas that live on the rats do.

• Don't worry if people don't want to speak to you. Everyone is so scared—some parents have even abandoned their sick children to avoid being infected themselves.

RUNNING SCARED

At the side of the road, you see a man running along with his face covered. When you go over to speak to him, he looks very afraid. However, once you have assured him that you are not infected in any way, he lets you accompany him to his house. His name is Giovanni. He apologizes for his rudeness, but explains that so many people have died from the disease everyone is now terrified. People are too scared to look after their loved ones when they are sick, or even bury them when they die.

So far, nobody has found a way to stop the disease. Some people have barricaded themselves in their homes. They believe the plague is a curse from God, and that by living well and praying, they will escape. Other people have left the city altogether in the hope that they can outrun the disease. A few people seem to have gone mad, trying to have as much fun as possible. They drink and eat as much as they like, and steal from people's abandoned homes.

They believe these are going to be their last days, so they are going to try to enjoy them as much as they can.

MEDIEVAL MEDICINE

Giovanni has seen many people die from the disease and hasn't yet seen a treatment that has worked. Here are some of the crazy cures people have tried:

- Bloodletting. This involves cutting the body and letting the infected blood run out. This does not work and will only make the patient weaker and more likely to die.

- Cutting open the swellings caused by the disease and putting dried toads on them to draw out the poison. This would probably only result in the wounds becoming infected.

- Holding a garland of strongly scented flowers and herbs. This might block out the smell of rotting corpses, but it won't stop people from being infected. They are infected not by the foul smell, but by the bites of infected fleas. A bunch of flowers isn't going to ward off fleas.

Giovanni stops at a door and knocks. It opens slightly and someone inside asks if he is alone. He says no and explains that you look perfectly healthy and are a traveler from a neighboring town. There is a commotion inside and a lot of shouting. Your friend apologizes to you, but then pushes himself through the door and slams it in your face.

You look down the street and it looks completely empty. Time to go, there's nothing left for you to do here—EJECT.

SICKLY SYMPTOMS WARNING

Phew! You're back in the present. Your TT handset is equipped with an ImmunoShield (see page 4), which protects you from catching the diseases of the past and stops you giving modern coughs and colds to the people you meet. However, in the rare event of a malfunction, look out for the following symptoms over the next few weeks:

• An itchy, black, pus-filled spot. This is an infected flea bite and may mean you are infected with the most common type of plague—bubonic plague. This can occur up to a week after having been bitten.

• Swellings in your armpit or groin. These are called buboes and can grow to be the size of an apple. Buboes are a sure sign that you have been infected by bubonic plague. The swellings are, in fact, your lymph nodes (organs in your body that work to fight against disease).

• An unusual rash without buboes. This could be a sign of septicemic plague. This is when the body is completely overwhelmed with plague bacteria and is always fatal.

• Coughing up blood and a high temperature. Take care because you may have caught an even more fast-acting form of the disease, pneumonic plague. This is when the plague bacteria has been transmitted in the coughed-up blood of other people and is now in your lungs.

If you feel at all unwell, seek medical attention. Modern antibiotics have proven very effective in treating the disease.

AD 100

HOW TO ROAST A RODENT WITH A ROMAN

You have landed on a long, dusty road in Northern Italy. Behind you, you hear the loud *crunch, crunch, crunch* of marching soldiers coming toward you. Eek! It sounds like the whole Roman army is at your back. As you turn around, the crunching comes to an abrupt halt. Mistaking you for one of the soldiers in his century, or unit of 80 men, the centurion, or leader of the century, tells you to get in line with the rest of the soldiers.

A LUCKY ESCAPE

You get in line next to a soldier named Curtius Balbas. He tells you that you are very lucky to get off so lightly. Punishments in the Roman legions are very harsh. Soldiers who misbehave are flogged and if the centurion had suspected you of making a run for it, every tenth man in the whole century could have been killed. This is called *decimatio* and the centurions use this as a warning to anyone wanting to flee from battle. Curtius says he has seen this happen before and that it is terrifying waiting to find out if it is going to be your turn for the sword.

LIFE IN THE LEGIONS

Today, the soldiers are on a training march. They do this three to four times a month and travel at speeds of up to 5 miles an hour and cover up to 25 miles in just five hours wearing full armor. In addition, they have to carry all the things they will need to set up camp. Curtius says that training is hard, but that it is much better than fighting or building long, straight roads like the one you are walking on now. Curtius has fought in 15 campaigns since he was called to serve when he was just 17 years old.

A GOOD MEAL

By the time you stop to make camp for the night, you are very tired. You are so hungry you could eat a horse, but Curtius has something much smaller in mind. He suggests feasting on a highly prized Roman delicacy—roasted dormouse. Dormice would usually be served at elegant banquets, but luckily for you, he keeps a jar with live dormice in it and offers them up for the meal. Not wanting to sound chicken, you accept his offer and watch how he prepares his Roman rodent recipe.

DELICIOUS DORMOUSE DELIGHT

In the present, the dormouse is an endangered species in its native England. Curtius uses real dormice for his recipe but he says you could use chicken pieces instead. ALWAYS cook with an adult and ask permission to use the oven.

You will need:
- 3 skinless, boneless chicken breasts
- 1 cup of Italian-seasoned bread crumbs
- ½ cup Parmesan cheese • 1 teaspoon salt
- 1 teaspoon thyme • 1 teaspoon dried basil
- ½ cup butter/margarine, melted

1. Preheat the oven to 400 degrees.

2. Cut chicken breasts into 1½-inch size pieces. In a medium bowl, mix together bread crumbs, Parmesan cheese, salt, thyme, and basil. Mix well. Put melted butter/margarine in a bowl for dipping.

3. Dip chicken pieces into the melted butter/margarine first, then coat with bread crumb mixture. Place well-coated chicken pieces on a lightly greased cookie sheet in a single layer, and bake in the preheated oven for 20 minutes.

Serves six hungry Romans.

HOW TO FOLLOW
THE OLD SILK ROAD

Ouch, you've landed right between two humps on a camel's back and it hurts! It's hard to say who is more surprised, you or the camel. But there's no time to think about that, because the camel is already moving. You're off along the Old Silk Road, the ancient trading route between China and Europe.

It's not like any road you know—more like a dusty track—and you're traveling with a caravan, or group of merchants, and their camels. They are taking silk, tea, porcelain, and other goods to trade with European merchants at trading posts and bazaars along the route. In exchange, your merchants will buy European goods such as gold, wool, and wine and take them back to China.

BANDITS

Be warned. The Old Silk Road goes through huge deserts and some of the highest mountain ranges in the world, and it's tough and dangerous to travel. You're traveling through bandit country, so watch out for ambushes. Likely places are narrow passes, dense undergrowth, and behind hilltops and large boulders. To make it harder for bandits, you can:

- Vary the speed at which you travel.

- Stop regularly, and check the route ahead and behind you.

- Keep an eye out for glints of light—it may be sunlight reflecting off something metal belonging to a crouching bandit.

- Make sure the members of your caravan are spaced out. You should aim to be close enough to help each other out, but far enough apart so that bandits can't completely surround you.

SANDSTORMS

You're in sandstorm country, too. Strong winds blowing over loose sand or soil create enormous dust clouds that move at speeds of up to 100 miles per hour. If you spot one, here's what to do:

- Move to higher ground if you can.

- Cover your nose and mouth with a wet cloth.

- Try to take shelter. Look for a large rock to protect you from the worst of the sand. Alternatively, use your new friend, your camel. Make it sit down, and squeeze down next to it on the side sheltered from the wind. Your camel will be all right. It has good protection against sandstorms. It can close its nostrils, and it has bushy eyebrows and long eyelashes to keep sand out of its eyes.

• Wrap yourself in anything you can to shield yourself. The strong winds may have scooped up heavy objects and you could be hit.

• Once the storm reaches you, stay put until it's over—visibility can be reduced to zero within seconds.

VERTIGO

When you reach the mountains, you'll be traveling along steep, narrow tracks with terrifying drops into ravines hundreds of yards below. If you are panicking, don't fight it. Accept that you're scared stiff. Slow down your breathing. Keep right behind the trader in front of you and follow in his camel's footsteps exactly. Look out for loose ground that could trip you up. Don't look too far ahead. Concentrate on here and now, and stop worrying about that even steeper part you can see ahead.

HOW TO GO WILD IN THE WEST

AD 1880

Aaaaargh! You've just landed in the middle of a river. It's icy cold. Your teeth are too frozen to even chatter. The river is wide and fast-flowing, and though it is quite shallow, the current is almost strong enough to whisk you off your feet. You grab hold of the nearest thing—an ox.

The ox is not alone. It's part of a team pulling a wagon across the river. There are more wagons up ahead, and still more behind you. In fact, there are wagons as far as your eyes can see in both directions. You have arrived in the middle of a long train of wagons heading westward. They are filled with people who have decided to leave the towns and cities in eastern America and travel to the west in search of a new and better life. This is the west we call the Wild West!

MAKING CAMP

Your TT handset may have state-of-the-art waterproofing, but you don't. You are drenched by the time you wade to the far bank. Luckily, the wagon master who is leading the train decides this is a good spot to make camp for the night.

Soon, all the wagons are arranged in a great big circle. Campfires are lit and big pots of food are cooking. You sit around the fire with your fellow travelers, singing songs and chatting under the stars. This most definitely beats your average camping vacation!

IT'S TOUGH OUT WEST

Don't be fooled by the campfire songs—the people singing are pioneers, and they are tough, because life in the west is tough.

- They start their day early, lighting fires and getting breakfast made before dawn.

- People have to walk most of the day. The oxen are already pulling heavy loads, and the terrain is bumpy. Riding in the wagons is no fun, either. You would be shaken like a rag doll, and all the pots and pans banging together makes a clanking racket.

- Despite being on the trail for ten or more hours, most wagon trains can only travel about 12 miles a day. If it's rainy and muddy, they manage a lot less.

- The children have lots of chores—such as collecting wood, helping cook, fetching water from the river, and milking cows.

DANGERS ON THE TRAIL

Heading west can be a dangerous journey. Keep a lookout for some of the potential perils ahead.

- The trail itself is full of danger. Some of the trail is through high mountain passes and across rivers far wider, deeper, and wilder than the one you just crossed.

- The Wild West is full of wildlife. There are rattlesnakes around whose bite could kill you. Wild dogs called coyotes and other savage animals roam in the night looking for a meal.

- The sun is very hot and the ground is very dry. Grass fires can flare up at any time and can engulf slow-moving wagons.

- The prairies are very open and exposed. During storms, a lightning strike can set a wagon on fire in seconds.

- The pioneers are carrying everything they own, so these slow-moving caravans are easy targets for bandits. Bandits and outlaws are a constant threat, and they are what make the West so wild.

FOLLOWING THE TRAIL

After a night sleeping by the campfire, you wake for another day on the trail. You decide to catch up to the wagon master at the head of the train. He gives the order for the wagons to move on. As you go along, he shows you some of the signs a wagon train in front has left behind. At first, they just look like piles of pebbles, but as you look more closely, he explains that these piles of pebbles show you which way to go and give warnings of any dangers that lie ahead.

He asks you to help him by setting signs along the trail for the pioneers trailing behind to follow. He tells you some of the different signs he uses.

STRAIGHT AHEAD

TURN LEFT

TURN RIGHT

NOT THIS WAY

DANGER

MESSAGE HIDDEN (STONES SHOW HOW MANY PACES TO TAKE TO FIND THE MESSAGE)

This is what the symbols on page 102 mean.

HEAD WALK WATER

HOW TO FLY IN A HOT-AIR BALLOON

The sound of roaring hot air burners fills your ears and you find yourself in the basket of a hot-air balloon soaring a thousand yards above the ground. You are not in just any balloon, you are taking part in the first-ever manned balloon flight.

There are two other people on board, a science teacher and an adventurer. After their initial shock on seeing you appear beside them, they tell you how the balloon was launched from the yard of a huge house just outside Paris. It is now soaring over the city, and has traveled about six miles, which is impressive when you consider no one has traveled through the air like this before. Below, people look like ants, cheering and waving. You wave back, enjoying your celebrity moment.

The huge balloon measures 25 yards tall and 15 yards across, with a fancy sky-blue and gold design all over it. It is made of a material called taffeta that has been covered with a fireproofing varnish. Unfortunately, the fireproofing isn't really working. You can smell burning. The balloon is starting to look a bit scorched. One of the men whips off his coat and beats the flame licking up at the taffeta balloon. It is time to land.

BALLOONING BROTHERS

You touch down between two windmills—and just in time—your TT handset is beginning to melt around the edges. Two brothers, Joseph and Etienne Montgolfier, are introduced to you. They are the brains behind this flight. Etienne has the business brain and Joseph is the mad inventor. Joseph tells you the idea for building the balloon you have just been traveling in came to him when he noticed how clothes drying over a fire billowed upward. After five years of experimenting, *voilà*, he built this big balloon.

Joseph admits that you and your two companions aren't the first living creatures to make a balloon flight. That honor went to a sheep, a duck, and a rooster who were sent on an earlier flight, but no one really knows what they thought of the experience.

Time to go. You sneak off behind a tree to activate the EJECT button on your singed TT handset—just imagine how much Joseph Montgolfier would like to get his hands on a machine that flies you through time as well as space....

THE TIMELINE

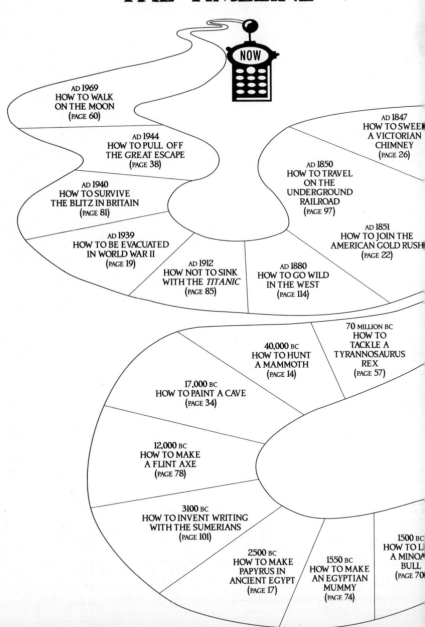

NOW

The LEAP button on your TT handset carries you back in time at random. However, if you wanted to travel back following the historical order in which the events in this book happened, this timeline shows you the route you would travel. It starts from the present day and ends up back in the time of the dinosaurs.

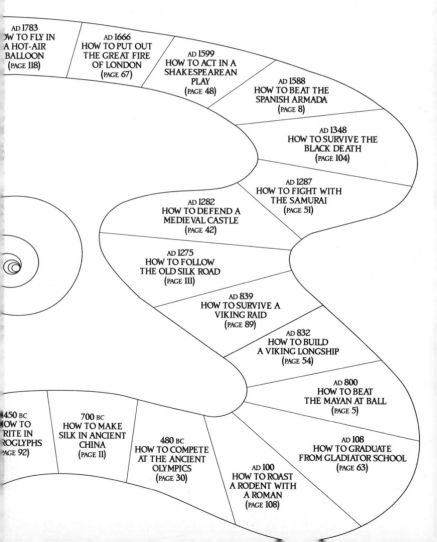

AD 1783
OW TO FLY IN
A HOT-AIR
BALLOON
(PAGE 118)

AD 1666
HOW TO PUT OUT
THE GREAT FIRE
OF LONDON
(PAGE 67)

AD 1599
HOW TO ACT IN A
SHAKESPEAREAN
PLAY
(PAGE 48)

AD 1588
HOW TO BEAT THE
SPANISH ARMADA
(PAGE 8)

AD 1348
HOW TO SURVIVE THE
BLACK DEATH
(PAGE 104)

AD 1287
HOW TO FIGHT WITH
THE SAMURAI
(PAGE 51)

AD 1282
HOW TO DEFEND A
MEDIEVAL CASTLE
(PAGE 42)

AD 1275
HOW TO FOLLOW
THE OLD SILK ROAD
(PAGE 111)

AD 839
HOW TO SURVIVE A
VIKING RAID
(PAGE 89)

AD 832
HOW TO BUILD
A VIKING LONGSHIP
(PAGE 54)

AD 800
HOW TO BEAT
THE MAYAN AT BALL
(PAGE 5)

AD 108
HOW TO GRADUATE
FROM GLADIATOR SCHOOL
(PAGE 63)

1450 BC
OW TO
RITE IN
ROGLYPHS
AGE 92)

700 BC
HOW TO MAKE
SILK IN ANCIENT
CHINA
(PAGE 11)

480 BC
HOW TO COMPETE
AT THE ANCIENT
OLYMPICS
(PAGE 30)

AD 100
HOW TO ROAST
A RODENT WITH
A ROMAN
(PAGE 108)